*Marguerite M. Coke, DSW*
*James A. Twaite, PhD, EdD*

# The Black Elderly: Satisfaction and Quality of Later Life

"**A** review of Social Work Abstracts lists a large number of articles on the elderly but few citation on the black elderly. Drs. Coke and Twaite's forthcoming book meets an ongoing need for more research and publications on the black elderly.

In their discussion of life satisfaction among the black elderly, they review the available literature, develop a comprehensive model for predicting life satisfaction and test the model among elderly blacks.

This book will be important for those working with the black elderly, graduate and undergraduate students, and faculty and directors of programs for the elderly. The book provides knowledge and information about the black elderly that is not readily available.

Finally, it affirms the role of the black church, its importance as an institution in black communities, and its role as a resource to social services providers and local and state policy makers who must address the provision of services to the black elderly."

**E. Aracelis Francis, DSW**
*Director, Minority Fellowship Programs,*
*Council on Social Work Education,*
*Alexandria, Virginia*

"**H**ooray for the black elderly, and congratulations to Marguerite Coke and James Twaite for their informative, yet easy-to-read, analytical assessment of black elderly life! Realistic in its presentation, this book makes the case for more research and studies that distinctly focus on the subjective well-being of elderly black Americans.

Most importantly, Coke and Twaite examine the lives of the black elderly from a positive and productive approach. They state the case, quite directly, for self-reporting methodology related to health and other variables, and their objective correlates. This book takes a significant and proactive look at how culture, church, and family solidify life among the black elderly, a diverse and complex group rich in tradition.

Policy recommendations are clear, forthright and sensible, placing them in a context that if followed will insure greater service provision and capacity for black seniors. A different perspective is given, and a wonderful assessment made, especially in terms of the multivariate model for predicting life satisfaction among elderly blacks.

A must read for those interested in championing the cause of the black elderly!"

**Steve Stitt, CSW**
*Psychotherapist/Hypnotherapist*
*in private practice,*
*New York City*

"**C**oke and Twaite have presented a thorough discussion of demographic and historical factors that influence the quality of life of the black elderly and have developed a comprehensive model of life satisfaction in this population. Readers will benefit from the discussion of the life satisfaction correlates of health status, income, education, and occupation, as well as the historical content pertaining to the family and church. The application of role theory to the information about the relationship of contemporary black elderly to their families is particularly illuminating.

Coke and Twaite have developed a model for predicting life satisfaction that draws upon relevant research and data collection in which they secured information from participants at a large number of senior centers. Their interpretation of the data is analytical, and their findings related to gender differences in religiosity and family role involvement are particularly informative. The policy implications will be helpful to planners and other service providers who want to implement services that facilitate the involvement of elderly blacks in activities that will be meaningful to them."

**Patricia Kolb, PhD**
*Education Coordinator,*
*Social Work Department,*
*Jewish Home and Hospital,*
*New York City*

The Haworth Press, Inc.

# The Black Elderly
## *Satisfaction and Quality of Later Life*

# HAWORTH Social Work Practice
## Carlton E. Munson, DSW, Senior Editor

New, Recent, and Forthcoming Titles:

*Management and Information Systems in Human Services: Implications for the Distribution of Authority and Decision Making* by Richard K. Caputo

*The Creative Practitioner: Creative Theory and Method for the Helping Services* by Bernard Gelfand

*Social Work Theory and Practice with the Terminally Ill* by Joan K. Parry

*Social Work in Health Settings: Practice in Context* by Toba Schwaber Kerson and Associates

*Gerontological Social Work Supervision* by Ann Burack-Weiss and Frances Coyle Brennan

*Group Work: Skills and Strategies for Effective Interventions* by Sondra Brandler and Camille P. Roman

*If a Partner Has AIDS: Guide to Clinical Intervention for Relationships in Crisis* by R. Dennis Shelby

*Social Work Practice: A Systems Approach* by Benyamin Chetkow-Yanoov

*Elements of the Helping Process: A Guide for Clinicians* by Raymond Fox

*Clinical Social Work Supervision, Second Edition* by Carlton E. Munson

*Intervention Research: Design and Development for the Human Services* edited by Jack Rothman and Edwin J. Thomas

*Forensic Social Work: Legal Aspects of Professional Practice* by Robert L. Barker and Douglas M. Branson

*Now Dare Everything: Tales of HIV-Related Psychotherapy* by Steven Dansky

*Building on Women's Strengths: A Social Work Agenda for the Twenty-First Century* by Liane V. Davis

*People with HIV and Those Who Help Them: Challenges, Integration, Intervention* by R. Dennis Shelby

*The Black Elderly: Satisfaction and Quality of Later Life* by Marguerite M. Coke and James A. Twaite

# The Black Elderly
## *Satisfaction and Quality of Later Life*

Marguerite M. Coke, DSW
James A. Twaite, PhD, EdD

The Haworth Press
New York • London

The Haworth Press, Inc., 10 Alice Street, Binghamton, NY 13904-1580

**Library of Congress Cataloging-in-Publication Data**

Coke, Marguerite M.
   The Black elderly : satisfaction and quality of later life / Marguerite Coke, James Twaite.
      p.   cm.
   Includes bibliographical references and index.
   ISBN 1-56024-914-5 (alk. paper)
   1. Afro-American aged–Attitudes. 2. Afro-American aged–Social conditions. 3. Aged–Social networks–United States. 4. Satisfaction. I. Twaite, James A., 1946-   . II. Title.
HQ1064.U5C524    1995
305.26′089′96073–dc20                                                                94-33089
                                                                                          CIP

# CONTENTS

# ABOUT THE AUTHORS

**Marguerite Coke, DSW,** is Director of the Graduate Program in Gerontology/Psychology at the College of New Rochelle in New York. Previously, she served as Director of the Bronx Field Office of the New York City Department for the Aging.

**James A. Twaite, PhD, EdD,** is in Private Practice as a Consulting Psychologist specializing in empirical research. He has doctoral degrees in Econometrics and Counseling Psychology and is the author of *Introductory Statistics* (Scott-Foresman, 1979).

# Preface

The proportion of the population of the United States who are over the age of 65 has been increasing rapidly and will continue to increase during the twenty-first century. The "greying" of the American people will place new demands on society in general and the social service delivery community in particular. In order to enhance the physical, emotional, and subjective well-being of older Americans, services of all kinds will need to be expanded. These services will need to address not only such basic needs as food, shelter, and medical care, but also less tangible needs for social intercourse, intellectual stimulation, and continuing active participation in society.

In order to plan programs that optimize the use of scarce resources, social policy planners must have an understanding of the factors that predict the satisfaction and well-being of seniors. Planners must also be aware of the extent to which such factors are provided through naturally occurring support systems within the community, such as extended family networks and the church. Failure to recognize such supports may lead to unnecessary and wasteful duplication of services. In contrast, the recognition of such naturally occurring support systems may lead to great savings, since these systems can be used to facilitate service delivery and increase service utilization.

Cultural differences are reflected in the kinds of natural support systems that are available to older individuals in different communities. The supports available to black, white, and Hispanic seniors may be quite different. Differences may also be associated with religious affiliation, nationality subgroup membership, and the type of community in which one resides. It is therefore important to understand the correlates of life satisfaction among various cultural groups.

Although a substantial amount of research has been conducted on the correlates of life satisfaction among elderly individuals in general, relatively little research has been done focusing on specific cultural groups. In particular, little research has been conducted to date on life satisfaction among elderly blacks. Given the substantial obstacles faced by elderly blacks in the form of poverty, health concerns, and continuing discrimination, the factors that promote life satisfaction among this group are particularly worthy of study.

The work presented here represents an attempt to develop and test a model for the prediction of life satisfaction among elderly blacks. An extensive review of the literature was utilized to identify potential predictor variables, and a large scale empirical research study was used to test the resulting model. The study results clearly suggest the importance of family role involvement and church activity as predictors of life satisfaction among elderly black Americans. On the basis of these findings recommendations are made regarding service delivery for this population. It is hoped that this study will provide valuable data to those responsible for developing social policy. It is also hoped that this work will inspire other investigators to examine in greater detail the correlates of life satisfaction among elderly blacks and among elderly citizens from various ethnic and cultural groups.

*Marguerite M. Coke*
*James A. Twaite*

# Acknowledgements

It is difficult yet gratifying to acknowledge those who in one way or another assisted in the development of this book. It is a pleasure to recognize colleagues and friends who have influenced the entire process of the completion of the book. I would like to acknowledge and recognize teachers and colleagues who encouraged me to aspire and challenged me to think. I owe thanks to Rubi Preston, James Twaite, Elizabeth Daise, Larcey McCarley, Eugene S. Callender, Dave Deochand, and Beverly Anderson.

Without my family, Henry Maxwell, Martha Coke, Marion Robinson, and my deceased stepfather, the writing of this book would have been difficult.

Finally, I would like to recognize all those who worked to make this book a reality: my colleague and Dean, Dr. Laura Ellis, for constant encouragement; my faculty, Dr. Ken Doka, Dr. Jim Magee, who encouraged this book; Dr. Elaine Norman, Dr. Gloria Donatello, Ms. J. E. Franklin, and The College of New Rochelle Administration.

Sincere thanks also to my secretarial help, Jen Ryan, who labored in preparing the manuscript in a creative and timely fashion; Rosemary Strobel, the Human Services Division secretary, who handled correspondence and calls, and finally to my co-author, Dr. James Twaite.

# Chapter 1

# Introduction

The status of elderly blacks has been described as reflecting the "double jeopardy" associated with being old as well as black (Dowd & Bengtson, 1978; Jackson, 1970, 1971; National Urban League, 1964). Like all older individuals in Western industrial nations, elderly blacks are confronted by negative attitudes toward old people (Cowgill & Holmes, 1972). However, elderly blacks also experience the economic and social difficulties associated with their status as members of a minority group, including poverty and illness.

## *SOCIOECONOMIC INDICATORS*

Taylor and Chatters (1988) reviewed the available data on socioeconomic status and concluded that aged blacks are much worse off than aged whites on a variety of indicators. Elderly blacks have lower incomes than their white counterparts, as well as lower levels of educational attainment, and lower occupational status. Manuel (1986) reported that in 1984 the median annual income among black males over the age of 65 was $6,163. This is 57 percent of the median income of white males over 65 ($10,890). The situation is similar for women. Black women over the age of 65 had a median annual income of $4,345 in 1984, representing about 69 percent of the median income of their white counterparts ($6,297). Based on data contained in the

1980 census, the New York City Department for the Aging concluded that 26 percent of elderly blacks in New York City were below the poverty line (DFTA, 1985).

More recent data suggest that this disparity has continued. A Census Bureau report issued in 1988 indicated that the median annual family income among elderly whites increased during the 1987 calendar year, but that among elderly blacks decreased (reported in *Christianity Today*, Oct. 21, 1988).

Other investigators have shown that older blacks do not have as much education as older whites (Taylor & Taylor, 1982; U.S. Bureau of the Census, 1983). Census data indicate that nearly 38 percent of black men over the age of 65 had completed less than five years of education, compared to fewer than 8 percent of white men.

Low levels of income and education are associated with inadequate housing and poor health (Hill, 1978; Jackson, 1985). Wright, Creecy, and Berg (1979) reported that among low income elderly blacks significant predictors of underutilization of medical services included the lack of availability of such services within a reasonable distance from home, the lack of insurance coverage, and the lack of money to pay for services. A number of other investigators have reported research suggesting that elderly blacks do not enjoy the same level of health as their white counterparts.

Dowd and Bengtson (1978) surveyed 1,269 Anglo, Mexican, and African-American elderly in Los Angeles and concluded that the Anglo respondents were in better health than respondents from either of the two minority groups. Cantor (1974) conducted a similar study of older individuals in New York and obtained similar results. Morrisson (1982) reported that blacks have lower life expectancies than whites, although he noted the existence of a "crossover" effect, such that black males who do reach the age of 65 tend to live longer than their white peers. The same effect occurs among black females at the age of 75.

Moore (1991) noted that the chronic medical problems that characterize the black elderly may have implications that extend beyond physical health. He found that physical illnesses were associated with psychological depression among the black elderly. This relationship may result from the fact that physical illnesses limit participation in certain work and social roles that provide purpose and meaning to the lives of older blacks.

## *COPING*

In spite of the clearly disadvantaged position in society of elderly blacks, several researchers have suggested that older blacks tend to have effective coping strategies which they use to reduce the stress associated with their disadvantaged status. Clavon and Smith (1986) interviewed 40 elderly blacks and reported that 32 of these individuals (80 percent) felt that they were doing well and had a positive sense of well-being. Only eight members of their sample felt unable to cope with the inequalities that they had experienced during their lives in the areas of income, health, housing, and employment. Clavon and Smith reported that in order to maintain an adequate income level, many of the individuals in their sample continued to work on a full-time or at least a part-time basis even after retiring from their primary careers. Clavon and Smith also reported that their respondents remained active in their communities and relied heavily on their religious beliefs for personal support and life satisfaction.

Allen and Chin-Sang (1990) elicited personal narratives from 30 elderly black women. These narratives were focused on the women's work histories and the meaning of leisure. The narratives revealed that most of the women had begun to work in childhood and had worked continuously through their lives in agricultural, domestic, or service industry jobs. Also, most continued after retirement to do volunteer work or to be self-employed. The investigators found that the women tended to choose leisure pursuits that reflected "their lifelong involvement in work and in the particular way that black women have provided services for others" (p. 740). The women perceived caregiving activities, including food shopping, cooking, and babysitting, as leisure activities. They perceived church activities as neither work nor leisure activity, but rather as a uniquely rewarding service activity. These findings may help to explain why elderly blacks can view their lives as satisfying in the absence of sufficient wealth to allow them to pursue such leisure activities as travel and sports. It appears that the population of elderly black provides validation for the theory that work and service have their own intrinsic rewards.

This finding is reinforced by the results of several studies that indicate that elderly blacks are far more likely than their white counterparts to make use of informal family and community support systems to cope with life stresses (Chatters, Taylor, & Neighbors, 1989; Krishef & Yoelin, 1981; Usui, 1984). Krishef and Yoelin (1981) compared elderly black and white residents of northern Florida with respect to the use of formal and informal supports to accomplish various life tasks. They found that blacks were significantly more likely that their white counterparts to employ informal supports with respect to transportation, income support, and the procurement of health care.

Gibson (1982, 1987) has reported the results of several large sample empirical investigations of the coping mechanisms employed by older black Americans. Her 1982 study employed data on black ( N = 1931 ) and white ( N = 20,317) individuals aged 60 and over who were surveyed by the Institute for Social Research at the University of Michigan. Each sample was described as a national probability sample representative of the elderly black and white populations of the nation. When the samples were compared on background and demographic data, the results indicated that the black seniors were poorer, less educated, and less apt to be married than their white counterparts.

These respondents were surveyed regarding how they handled matters that were bothering them. They were also asked if they talked the problems over with anyone and, if so, with whom. When responses were analyzed, seven response categories were constructed, as follows: (1) informal help seeking; (2) religious means (of which prayer was the primary means cited); (3) denial; (4) displacement; (5) passive reactions; (6) independent coping reactions; and (7) "other" actions, including sleep, drinking alcohol, fantasy, and taking medication. Those respondents who mentioned that they received informal help were further categorized with respect to the source of the assistance. The four categories constructed for this purpose were: (1) spouse only; (2) single family member other than spouse; (3) multiple family members; and (4) friends.

The results indicated that black and white respondents were about equally likely to use informal help-seeking to cope with difficulties. However, the two groups differed significantly and substantially in the specific categories of individuals from whom help was sought. The elderly white respondents were more likely to report that they sought help from their spouses only or from a single family member. In contrast, the elderly black respondents were more likely to seek help from friends and from combinations of family members. These differences remained significant after the effects of age, income, and number of adults living in the respondent's household were controlled. These findings were interpreted as supporting the notion that elderly blacks rely more heavily than elderly whites on an extended family network.

The results of the study also indicated that black respondents were significantly more likely than white respondents to respond to difficult situations with prayer. In fact, prayer was the modal self-reported coping modality among black respondents. Nearly 55 percent of the elderly black in the sample indicated that they found relief from worry through prayer. This finding was interpreted in the context of suicide rates among black and white elderly. Gibson (1982) pointed out that elderly black women have the lowest suicide of any elderly group, whereas elderly white males have the highest rate. She noted that elderly black women are also the most likely to report coping through the use of prayer, whereas elderly white men are the least likely to do so. Gibson did not attribute this relationship to divine intervention. Instead, she referred to Durkeim's theory that suicide tends to be the lowest among those who are most strongly bonded to groups. That is, the stronger the social integration in a particular group, the less likely individuals are to commit suicide. Gibson noted further that blacks frequently pray together in times of need. She suggested that it may well be the communal aspect of prayer, the sense of prayer as a source of social support, that provides the connection between religion and lower suicide rates among older black women. Thus the role of religion and the church as a source of support among black elderly should not be construed narrowly. It would appear that religion functions broadly as a vehicle through which additional support of a social and perhaps even economic nature can be secured. These issues will be considered in greater detail in subsequent chapters.

These reports suggest that elderly blacks are a highly resilient group who appear to be able to cope with the stresses associated with their disadvantaged status through a variety of strategies that include involvement in service to family and community, church participation, and reliance on informal supports. The available data also suggest that the coping strategies employed by elderly blacks may be substantially different from those employed by whites and members of other cultural groups. Therefore it would appear that in studying the factors that predict the subjective well-being of elderly citizens, blacks and whites should be studied as distinct groups.

## ECONOMIC TRENDS
## AND THE FUTURE OF THE BLACK ELDERLY

As the United States approaches the twenty-first century, several demographic and economic trends are combining to render the status of elderly blacks even more tenuous that it has been until this time. Markides and Levin (1987) pointed out that the economic and occupational structures of urban America have changed dramatically over the past several decades. The urban areas of this country are no longer the centers of production. Instead, the cities have become the centers of information, administration, and the provision of services (Kasarda, 1983). These changes have resulted in a loss to the cities of blue-collar jobs, which have shifted to outlying non-metropolitan areas.

But it is in the urban areas that the majority of minority group citizens live, including elderly blacks. Moreover, minority group members in general and elderly minority group members in particular tend to have relatively little education. Thus they tend not to be qualified for the higher level white collar jobs that are developing in the urban areas. Furthermore, the increase in the proportion of minority group members in the urban areas has led to the departure to the suburbs of many middle income individuals, along with the retail and service establishments that had previously existed to support these individuals. This trend results in a further erosion of blue collar and lower level white collar jobs that might otherwise be available to minority group members.

Markides and Levin (1987) noted that these shifts have resulted in a situation where white farmers in rural areas are now obtaining industrial jobs to replace or supplement their dwindling farm incomes, while inner city minority group members are effectively squeezed out of the job market. They noted that some inner city poor with automobiles actually do make the daily commute to the suburbs for work, but most minority group members are not so fortunate. Furthermore, as industrial sites have dispersed throughout suburban and even rural areas, public transportation is most often not a viable option. Thus Kasarda (1983) estimated that 80 percent of inner city blacks in the Chicago area do not have access to any form of transportation to suburban job sites.

These trends led Markides and Levin to predict that elderly blacks in the next century will continue to grow old isolated from the economic mainstream of America. For this reason, they suggested that programs and support services designed to meet the needs of the black elderly will become even more important in the future than they are now.

## WHY STUDY THE BLACK ELDERLY?

The proportion of the total population of the U.S. who are over the age of 65 has been increasing rapidly. Clavon and Smith (1986) estimated that by the year 2030 nearly one-fifth of the total population of the United States would be over 65. Dillard, Campbell, and Chisolm (1984) provided an even higher estimate for the same time frame, suggesting that by 2030 approximately one American in four would be a senior citizen. In terms of absolute numbers, it is estimated that in 2030 there will be over 50 million elderly individuals in the U.S.

Mead (1970) suggested that in the United States old age is really viewed as a "form of illness to be lamented but not mentioned earlier than necessary" (p. 137). Among the reasons for this characterization of old age in America are the dominant cultural values of self-reliance and independence. When older individuals can no longer be self-reliant and independent, they tend to be stigmatized. However, the dominant cultural values within American society do not pertain equally to all groups in the society. In order to understand the experience of aging of a particular individual from any cultural group, it is necessary to understand the particular values of his or her culture that define the accepted roles of elderly persons in that community. Unfortunately, relatively little research has been carried out to date focusing on these cultural issues. Holzberg (1982) has argued that research on aging in general and even research on minority aging has tended to give inadequate attention to important cultural differences that may alter the experience of aging among different groups.

Specifically, Holzberg criticized the gerontological literature on aging for focusing almost entirely on the fact that minority elderly tend to be poor. She suggested that the literature leaves one with the impression that minority elderly are living in a "culture of poverty" that largely defines their experience of aging. This culture is viewed as including such factors as chronic unemployment, low wages, poor housing, feelings of fatalism and helplessness, and a strong tendency toward a present time orientation. A corollary of this conceptualization of the minority aging experience is that the culture of poverty is handed down from generation to generation. Holzberg argued that this view of minority aging confuses culture with social class and ignores other important aspects of culture that may impact on the aging process, including typical patterns of family relationships, attitudes toward the elderly, and accepted roles for the elderly within the family and community.

Holzberg recommended that research on minority aging needs to be focused more on the "internal protective structures and the adaptive cultural prescriptions not specifically related to the situational imperatives of poverty and racism" (1982, p. 251). Within this category of cultural factors Holzberg included life-styles, customs, primary interactional networks, perceptions, and attitudes toward the elderly. She also suggested that it was necessary to consider the heterogeneity that exists among ethnic populations. She argued that it is important to determine the manner in which ethnicity can facilitate or hamper successful adjustment to old age. This exploration requires researchers to identify ethnic communities that provide naturally occurring organized support systems such as voluntary associations, clinics, and information centers for the elderly. It also requires the identification within the various communities of cultural values that have an impact on the roles assumed by the elderly within the community. The work described here represents an effort to answer questions of this nature with respect to the black elderly. Future research will be required to address these issues for other ethnic and cultural groups. However, it makes good sense to focus initially on the black elderly, since the black elderly constitute an increasingly large proportion of the population of Americans over the age of 65.

Blacks will constitute approximately one-fifth of this huge population of elderly Americans. Over the past two decades the number of blacks who are over the age of 65 has increased by approximately 25 percent, more than double the rate of growth of the overall black population. Thus, over the next four decades, older persons in general and older blacks in particular will represent a considerably larger segment of American society. Wheeler (1986) has suggested that in order to provide better health care and social support to the black elderly, more research is required on how black peoples age, differences between blacks and whites with respect to the aging process, and factors associated with life satisfaction within this population. However, despite the large numbers of black elderly in our society and the predictions of growth among this group, relatively little research has been carried out on the black elderly. In particular only one recent study (Coke, 1991) has considered the correlates of life satisfaction among black senior citizens. More empirical work is required to identify those aspects of the lives of elderly blacks that are associated with their subjective well-being. The work reported here consists of a review of the available literature aimed at developing a comprehensive model for predicting the subjective well-being of elderly blacks, an empirical test of the resulting model, and a statement of the policy implications of the results.

Chapter 2

# Demographic Correlates
# of Life Satisfaction
# Among Elderly Blacks

The literature on life satisfaction among the elderly in general makes it clear that demographic factors, including health status, adequacy of income, and the related factors of educational and occupational level are correlates of life satisfaction. The literature on elderly blacks shows that these same variables are significant for blacks as well. This chapter reviews the empirical literature relevant to these factors.

## *HEALTH*

Chatters and Taylor (1989) studied the life problems of elderly blacks. They surveyed 581 blacks ages 55 or over. This group broke down as follows: 240 (41 percent) of the respondents were between 55 and 64; 230 (40 percent) were between 65 and 74; and 111 (19 percent) were 75 or older. These respondents were read a list of ten life domains and asked whether they had experienced any problems in any of these domains during the month before the survey. Respondents who indicated that they did have a problem in a particular domain were also asked to rate the degree of distress associated with the problem on a four-point Likert-type scale having response options ranging from "not at all" to "a great deal." The results of this study indicated that the area of health was both the most frequently mentioned problem area and the source of greatest distress. Sixty percent of respondents who indicated that they had problems in any of the ten areas indicated that they had a health-related problem in the previous month. This figure is impressive for two reasons. First, the period of one month before the survey is relatively brief, leading one to suspect that an even higher figure might have been obtained had a period of six months or a year been used. Second, the sample employed in the study had a large proportion of respondents in the 55- to 64-year-old age group, who might be expected to have fewer health problems than those in the older age cohorts. Similarly, Wallace (1990a) concluded that the black elderly are significantly more likely than the white elderly to report poor or fair health status. These reports make it clear that health is perceived as a problem area by a substantial proportion of elderly blacks.

Researchers have also presented objective data indicating that elderly blacks do indeed have more health-related problems than their white peers. Clavon (1986) reported that 51 percent of all blacks who are 65 or older are limited in their major life activity (e.g., paid employment, keeping house) by some chronic health condition. The comparable figure among whites in the same age range is 36 percent. Wallace (1990a) also reported that black elderly are more likely than whites to experience limitations in the activities they can perform, and he suggested that such limitations are typically the result of chronic illnesses.

The health problems experienced by elderly blacks are made more serious by their tendency to underutilize health care delivery systems. Downing and Copeland (1980) suggested that blacks are likely to have to travel farther than their white counterparts to reach health care facilities. This problem is exacerbated by economic constraints faced by many elderly blacks, which may make travel to health care facilities prohibitively expensive. Downing and Copeland (1980) also argued that older blacks may be inhibited from using health care services, because facilities are often staffed primarily by white professionals who may appear intimidating and may lack the ability to communicate effectively with older blacks.

Others have attributed the underutilization of services to institutional discrimination. For example, Butler and Lewis (1982) have argued that nursing homes and homes for the aged are largely segregated, even though such policies are not stated explicitly. Wallace (1990b) reported the results of a study carried out in the St. Louis area that indicated patterns of institutional segregation with respect to both nursing homes and hospitals. Wallace employed data from 122 health care facilities that served predominantly adult populations. Wallace noted that "hospital data by race is not easily obtained. The state does not collect such data and the industry's data center refused to provide hospital level discharge data by race" (p. 518). Nevertheless, through the use of death rates among older persons as a proxy variable that is sensitive to the distribution of older persons by race within each hospital, Wallace was able to demonstrate patterns of segregation that could not be explained by economic barriers alone.

The strongest predictor of the proportion of African-Americans in a given health care facility was the proportion of African-Americans in the neighborhood where the facility was located. Wallace (1990b) suggested both a cultural and a racial theory to explain this finding. The cultural theory suggests that families tend to place their elderly in nursing homes and hospitals that are close to their homes, in order to make visiting easier. Racial theories suggest that the professional referral network steers African-Americans away from white nursing homes, and that African-Americans avoid the white neighborhoods of South St. Louis because of their racist reputations. Wallace gave special emphasis to the role of hospital discharge planners, since nursing homes obtain from 70 to 80 percent of their admissions through referrals from other institutions.

Another factor that contributes to the underutilization of health care services by the black elderly is the culturally based tendency of blacks to obtain assistance from nontraditional sources of support, including family and kinship networks (Adams, 1980; Wright, Creecy, & Berg, 1979). The value placed on "caring for our own" has a particularly strong negative impact on the utilization of nursing homes by black families (Clavon, 1986).

The disproportionately large number of health problems experienced by elderly blacks is extremely important, because both objective health status and self-perceptions of health are related strongly to psychological adjustment and subjective well-being. These relationships have been demonstrated for both the elderly in general and for the black elderly in particular.

Spreitzer and Snyder (1974) used data from the National Data Program for the Social Sciences at the National Opinion Research Center to determine the best predictors of life satisfaction among Americans over the age of 64. Self-assessed health was the strongest predictor of life satisfaction among this group, explaining 17 percent of the variance in the dependent measure.

Mancini (1981) examined the relationship between life satisfaction and self-rated health among a sample of 74 senior citizens who were residing in high-rise public housing complexes in a city in the southeast. He found that self-rated health was a significant predictor of life satisfaction among this group. Several other studies have yielded significant correlations between self-ratings of health and life satisfaction among the elderly (Tate, 1982; Usui, Keil, & Durig, 1985). Based on a review of the literature on factors related to life satisfaction among older adults, McGhee (1985) concluded that health status is consistently the most important predictor of psychological well-being.

Several studies have investigated the relationship between health and measures of psychological adjustment among elderly blacks. Husaini, Moore, Castor, Neser, Whitten-Stovall, Linn, and Grifen (1991) examined the relationship between medical problems and depression among 600 blacks ranging in age from 55 to 85. They measured chronic medical problems using a checklist of disorders. The list included "problems of all organ systems that are chronically affected by the aging process (e.g., heart diseases, diabetes, etc.)" (p. 237). Depression was measured by the Center for Epidemiologic Studies Depression (CES-D) Scale (Radloff, 1977). This scale measures depressive symptoms experienced during the week preceding the administration of the scale. The results indicated that the number of medical problems reported was related significantly to depression among both females (beta = .26, p < .05) and males (beta = .22, p < .05). Moreover, the mean number of chronic conditions reported was significantly (p < .05) higher among females (mean = 3.29) than among males (mean = 2.40). Females had a higher mean on depression (mean = 4.53) than males (mean = 2.40). However, the mean gender difference on depression was not significant. Neither group's mean approached the CES-D cut-off score signifying a clinically significant level of depression, 16.

Another study of black elderly (Coke, 1991) yielded opposite results with respect to the relationship between health and life satisfaction. Coke interviewed 166 blacks over the age of 64 who were residing in the borough of the Bronx, New York City. She assessed health status by a self-report scale asking respondents to indicate whether they would describe their health as poor, fair, good, or excellent. She measured life satisfaction using the five-item Diener subjective well-being scale (Diener, 1984). The results of this study indicated no significant relationship between self-rated health and life satisfaction among either males (r = .01, p > .05, *n* = 87) or females (r = −.05, p > .05, *n* = 79). Self-reported health did contribute to life satisfaction in a multiple regression analysis performed on the pooled sample of males and females (t = 2.03, p < .05). However, this finding was really an artifact resulting from significant differences between females and males on life satisfaction and self-rated health.

The most obvious explanation for the differences between the results of the studies by Husaini and his associates (1991) and Coke (1991) would appear to be the difference in the measurement of health. Whereas Husaini et al. employed a checklist of actual ailments, Coke used a single-item global self-report of general health. However, there is considerable theoretical literature suggesting that self-reports of health are valid indicators of psychological well-being, and there is considerable empirical data suggesting that self-reports of health are correlated significantly with objective measures of health status.

Liang (1986) proposed a model for evaluating health status consisting of three interrelated components: (1) the medical definition of health is based on the absence of disease. Appropriate measures of medical health include sick day, number of hospitalizations, and number of physical ailments. (2) The social definition of health has to do with the capacity of the individual to perform his or her designated social role responsibilities at an acceptable level. Logical measures of social health would include self-reports, reports of family members, and reports of employers. (3) Finally, Liang described the subjective model of health as "the individual's perception and evaluation of his or her overall physical health" (p. 249), often measured by a single four- or five-point scale having responses ranging from poor to excellent. Liang cited Tissue (1974) and Brook et al. (1979) as concluding that "an individual's self-rated health represents a summary statement concerning the ways in which various aspects of health, subjective as well as objective, are combined within one's perceptual framework" (1986, p. 249). Thus, Liang argued that the subjective self-report approach to the measurement of health was probably the most comprehensive.

Numerous studies have demonstrated significant empirical relationships between self-reports of overall health status and various objective measures that one would expect to be related to health. Tessler and Mechanic (1978) reported a significant correlation between self-rated health and psychological stress. They also noted that this relationship persisted even after physical measure of health and socio-demographic measures were controlled. Weinberger, Darnell, Martz, Hiner, Neill, and Tierney (1986) examined the relationship between self-reported health status and positive and negative life changes among a sample of 187 elderly residents of public housing units in Indianapolis. The sample was 49.7 percent black and 50.3 percent white. The results indicated a rather strong negative relationship between the number of negative life events during the previous year and self-ratings of health. In a related study, Weinberger, Darnell, Tierney, Martz, Hiner, Barker, and Neill (1986) assessed the validity of self-rated health in a one-year prospective study of 155 elderly public housing tenants. Results indicated that poor self-rated health was a significant risk factor for both hospital admission and nursing home placement. Other studies suggesting the validity of single-item subjective measures of health status have been reported by: LaRue, Bank, Jarvik, and Hetland (1987), who showed that self-rated health is related significantly to physician's ratings of health; Ferraro (1980), who reported significant relationships between self-reports of health and both extent of disability and number of illnesses; Linn and Linn (1980), who reported that self-rated health was correlated significantly with physician visits, hospitalization during the prior six-month period, diagnoses, use of medications, and impairment and disability ratings; and Mossey and Shapiro (1982), who reported a significant relationship between self-reported health and mortality.

In summary, the literature suggests that health is related to life satisfaction among both the general population of older adults and the black elderly. Moreover, there is considerable agreement that a single-item global self-report measure is a valid measure that encompasses the various domains of the health concept.

## SOCIOECONOMIC INDICATORS

After health, the most important demographic correlates of life satisfaction among the elderly are the socioeconomic indicators of income, education, and occupation. As indicated in the first chapter of this book, older blacks are clearly worse off with respect to socioeconomic status than older whites (Hill, 1978; Jackson, 1985; Taylor & Chatters, 1988; Taylor & Taylor, 1982). Some of the demographic data provided by Taylor and Chatters (1988) in their study of a national sample of 581 elderly black adults make clear the economic difficulties faced by the black elderly.

One fourth of their sample had annual household incomes of less than $5,000, and only 28 percent had annual household incomes over $12,000. Thirty-one percent of the sample was below the poverty line. Sixty-eight percent of the sample was not working. Only one fourth of the sample were high school graduates.

Spreitzer and Snyder's (1974) study of correlates of life satisfaction among the general population of older adults, based on a sample of 1,547 individuals, yielded significant correlations between life satisfaction and all three socioeconomic indicators: family income ($r = .13$, $p < .01$), educational level ($r = .10$, $p < .01$), and occupational level ($r = .11$, $p < .01$). Of course, these correlations are modest in magnitude, and they are significant beyond the .01 level because of the large sample size in this study. Spreitzer and Snyder (1974) also reported a correlation of .24 ($p < .01$) between life satisfaction and self-rated satisfaction with one's financial situation. That the correlation between life satisfaction and the subjective measure of financial satisfaction is stronger than the correlation between life satisfaction and actual income indicates that judgments regarding one's financial position may be relative rather than absolute.

The latter conclusion is supported by the research of Usui, Keil, and Durig (1985). These researchers obtained "micro-level socio-economic comparisons" from their respondents through questions concerned with how the financial situations of one's closest relative, closest neighbor, and closest friend compared with one's own (p. 111). Responses to such queries were made on five-point Likert-type response scales with response options ranging from "he/she is much better off" (1) to "he/she is much worse off" (5). Usui and his colleagues measured life satisfaction using the 13-item Life Satisfaction Index-Z (LSIZ; Neugarten, Havighurst, & Tobin, 1961). The results of the study indicated that relative income was not only a significant (p < .001) predictor of life satisfaction, but that it was a far stronger predictor than any of a series of objective measures including actual income, health, education, social contacts, and church attendance. However, educational level was correlated significantly to life satisfaction in this study.

A study reported by Tate (1982) provided still another perspective on the impact of finances on life satisfaction. Tate measured adverse changes in the financial situations of her sample of 30 black and 30 white women over the age of 65. Tate found that the presence of such changes was correlated negatively with life satisfaction measure by the Life Satisfaction Index (r = −.33, p < .01). Here again the result suggests that financial status is more significant when measured relative to the respondent's frame of reference than when measured in absolute terms. Tate also reported in this study that years of education were not correlated significantly with life satisfaction in this sample.

Coke's (1991) study (referred to previously) examined the relationship between self-perceived adequacy of income and life satisfaction. She measured adequacy of income using a single five-point Likert-type item having response options ranging from "not at all adequate" to "completely adequate." She reported a significant correlation between this measure and scores on Diener's subjective well-being scale (r = .23, p < .01). However, this significant correlation observed in the total sample was the result of the relationship between these variables among males ($r = .29$, $p < .01$, $n = 87$). The relationship between self-perceived adequacy of income and life satisfaction among women was not significant ($r = -.02$, $p > .05$, $n = 77$).

At least one study to date reported a nonsignificant relationship between income and life satisfaction. Mancini's (1981) study of 74 elderly residents of high-rise public housing units yielded a correlation of only .11 ($p > .05$) between actual yearly income and life satisfaction. It should be noted that this correlation is similar in magnitude to the correlation of .13 reported between income and life satisfaction by Spreitzer and Snyder (1974). That correlation was highly significant ($p < .01$) due to the large sample size they employed ($n = 1,547$). The similar correlation reported by Mancini (1981) was not significant with a sample size of 74.

Taken together, these data suggest that absolute measures of dollar income are less predictive of life satisfaction than relative and subjective measure of satisfaction with income.

# Chapter 3

# West African Culture, Slavery, and the Role of the Elderly in Black American Families

## *THE IMPACT OF AFRICAN CULTURE ON BLACKS IN AMERICA*

There has been substantial debate concerning the impact of African culture on blacks in the United States. In *Beyond the Melting Pot*, Glazer and Moynihan (1963) asserted that African-Americans did not have the same kind of historical and cultural tradition that other ethnic and cultural groups brought to the U.S. They suggested that American blacks have no unique history and culture to adhere to in the face of the onslaught of American culture. For this reason Glazer and Moynihan concluded that American blacks are only Americans and nothing else. Similarly, Frazier (1966) argued that the institution of slavery, wresting individuals from their homes and families and placing them in servitude in an alien culture, obliterated the influence of African culture on American blacks. On the other hand, Herskovitz (1958) has argued that significant aspects of West African culture survived to be reflected in the culture of blacks, including the areas of art, oral history, and family roles.

Billingsley (1992) has catalogued a number of the elements of African culture that have survived in America. These include: (1) the primacy accorded to blood ties over all other types of relationships, including marriage; (2) the importance of extended families versus nuclear families; and (3) the strong value placed on children. Billingsley highlighted the importance of the family among American blacks both before and after the demise of slavery.

Riley (1971) also considered the effect of slavery on the transmission of African cultural values to blacks in America. Riley argued that the importance of extended family or clan, the high regard for human life, and the reverence for old age and ancestors that characterized West African culture were all transmitted to the Americas more or less intact. Slavery had little effect on these cultural values, because slavers generally endeavored to take strong, mature individuals for the slave trade. They rarely took children. Thus the slaves that came to the Americas had been raised to adulthood in the cultural traditions of their tribes. Riley argued that it would have been impossible to break these traditions that had been inculcated over the course of a lifetime. Therefore West African values were translated into the new situations faced during slavery. In fact, Riley suggested that the value placed on family and the roles of women and the elderly was strengthened by the common suffering associated with slavery. The sections that follow consider each of these traditions.

## THE FAMILY

In West African society the family was an extended network of kinship involving reciprocal roles and responsibilities. According to Billingsley (1992), "marriage in the African tradition is not simply a union between two people but between groups of people. The kinship unit expands to embrace another whole set of kinfolk" (p. 28). Billingsley suggested that this aspect of marriage is still alive among black Americans. Although it is no longer necessary to secure the permission of parents for a woman and a man to marry, it is nevertheless the case that marriage is viewed as an event involving the support of both families.

White (1985) argued that the institution of marriage was particularly important among slaves: "African-Americans understood their family to be a haven in a heartless southland. It was within the slave family that a man, humiliated by the overseer's commands or lash, received respect. There, too, the overworked or brutally punished bondwoman received compassion" (p. 105). White noted that marriages among slaves tended to be stable and monogamous, and that the institution often served as a buffer to the callousness and insensitivity of the slave owner.

Broman (1988) reported the results of a large sample empirical study which suggested that both marital status and parenthood were important predictors of life satisfaction for black adults in general and for older blacks in particular. Broman's sample (N = 2,107) came from the National Survey of Black Americans (NSBA). The data were collected by the Survey Research Center at the University of Michigan during the period from 1979 to 1980. The sample represents a national cross-section of all blacks in the United States 18 years of age or older. Of the total sample, 440 respondents were age 60 years or above. The response rate for the survey was nearly 70 percent.

The results of the study indicated that life satisfaction was significantly higher among those who were married and widowed than among those who were single, divorced, or separated. Further, life satisfaction was higher among those respondents who indicated that they did not have children than among those who did have children. The finding obtained with respect to marital status was consistent across respondent gender and age group. Broman noted that this finding was similar to results reported earlier by Campbell, Converse, and Rodgers (1976), but contrary to results reported by Ball and Robbins (1986). Ball and Robbins found that marital status was related to life satisfaction for men only, and not for women. Moreover, Ball and Robbins reported that the relationship they observed for male black was exactly the opposite to that found by Broman. That is, Ball and

Robbins found that the black males with the highest measured life satisfaction were those who were divorced or separated. Broman explained this discrepancy by noting that the study reported by Ball and Robbins (1986) had been conducted in a rural area of Florida, whereas the Broman's data included representative proportions of urban and rural respondents of each gender. Moreover, Broman's data indicated an important effect of urbanicity on measured life satisfaction. Rural respondents were significantly higher on life satisfaction than were urban respondents.

Broman also pointed out another important factor that must be considered when evaluating the effect of marital status on life satisfaction. He noted that divorced people do not typically possess the same levels of social and emotional support that married people do. Divorced persons are not as likely as married individuals to name a person with whom they feel they can confide. Divorced persons tend to have smaller social networks. Divorced persons tend to report experiencing feelings of loneliness more frequently than married persons. Thus the effect of marital status observed by Broman may be due in part to the role of other factors that are correlated with marital status, rather than marital status *per se*. Nevertheless, there are numerous other sources in the literature that suggest that marriage and the family are extremely important for black Americans, including elderly blacks.

Billingsley (1992) argued that marriage remains a strong institution among contemporary black Americans. Contrary to the "vanishing black family" hypothesis, the vast majority of blacks live in families related by marriage, blood, or adoption. Moreover, the majority of these family households are married couple households. Finally, the majority of black married couples have young children of their own. Thus "marriage and family life are still important characteristics of the African-American community" (p. 207). Billingsley also emphasized the importance of the

institution of adoption among African-American families, a phe-
nomenon due in part to the strength of the extended family network. Billingsley concluded that the black extended family has
excelled particularly in the area of informal adoption: "Most
black children born out of wedlock are cared for by extended
families, generally their grandmothers, without the benefit of
legal adoption" (p. 30). This conclusion was supported by the
research of Hill (1977), who found that 90 percent of black
babies born out of wedlock are raised in three-generation families headed by grandparents.

Thus the West African tradition of kinship and marriage seems to
be reflected clearly in contemporary black America. Another aspect
of West African culture that has been transmitted to black American
culture is the importance of women and the maternal role.

## WOMEN AND MOTHERHOOD

White (1985) has concluded that "many slave mothers adhered
to mores that made motherhood almost sacred, mores rooted in the
black woman's African past" (p. 106). White explained that in
traditional West Africa motherhood and the nurturance of children
were highly valued roles. Mothers "ensured the survival of the
lineage, the consanguinal corporate group that controlled and dic-
tated the use and inheritance of property, provided access to various political and/or religious offices, regulated marriages, and performed political and economic functions" (p. 106). West Africa
had both matrilineal and patrilineal societies. In the matrilineal
societies, the mother's line determined inheritances, succession,
and citizenship, so the importance of the mother was evident. Even
in the patrilineal societies, however, mothers were viewed as important. A man's wife gave him children, and in agricultural societies the work of children translated directly into wealth. Children
were also heirs through which accumulated wealth and status
could be held within the family.

White noted that in many West African societies marriages were not considered consummated until after the birth of the couple's first child. In addition, the birth of the first child marked a transition from adolescence to adulthood for both husband and wife. Only after the birth of a man's first child could he establish his own household independent of that of his father, and only after the birth of the first child could a wife leave her family's home to take up residence with her husband.

The importance of the mother in traditional West African culture is also reflected in the care given to mothers when they became old. According to White, children represented a woman's most important "hedge against indigence" in her elderly years (p. 108). In West African society it was considered unthinkable for a child not to care for an elderly mother. However, it should be noted that the obligation to care for one's elderly mother is in part a function of the esteem accorded to the elderly in general, rather than simply a function of the maternal role. The section of this chapter that follows considers the transmission of the West African cultural tradition of veneration for the elderly.

## THE ELDERLY

Fortes (1950) described the veneration accorded the elderly in West African societies as resulting from the close relationships that existed between parents and children. According to Fortes, "the warmth, trust, and affection frequently found uniting parents and offspring go harmoniously with the respect shown to both . . . to insult, abuse, or assault one's father is an irreparable wrong; one which is bound to bring ill luck. While there is no legal obligation on a son or a daughter to support a father in his old age, it would be regarded as a shame and evil if he or she did not do so" (p. 235).

Lund, Feinhauer, and Miller (1985) attributed the veneration of the elderly in West African societies to their tradition of oral history. This tradition automatically gave the elderly a position of status, because old people were the repositories of the history, knowledge, and traditions of the culture. In addition, the recounting of historical tales would be expected to forge close relationships between the elderly storytellers and their young listeners.

Another factor related to the high status of the elderly in West African society is the common practice of ancestor worship among many cultural groups. In most West African cultures, groups of elders were accorded the honor of presiding over religious ceremonies and official functions. Riley (1971) noted that African culture views life and death along a continuum. Age was not viewed as a process that leads to the degeneration of mind and body, but rather as a source of knowledge, dignity, and respect. Thus the elders in African society were viewed traditionally as important, contributing members of society. Because the elders were viewed as closest to the venerated ancestors, they were accorded great respect.

## FAMILY ROLE RESPONSIBILITIES

The high status occupied by the elderly in West African societies is reflected today in America by the substantial involvement of the elderly in family role responsibilities. Because of the tradition of taking care of elderly family members, the elderly often reside with their married children in three-generation households. Furthermore, because of the respect accorded to the elderly, they are frequently given significant responsibility with respect to the care and upbringing of grandchildren.

A number of empirical studies have demonstrated that black American elderly are more likely than their white counterparts to perform important roles such as child care and involvement in the education of their grandchildren. Rubenstein (1972) reported that elderly blacks were more likely than elderly whites to live with their children in three-generation households, as opposed to living alone or living with a spouse only. This finding was replicated by Linn, Hunter, and Perry (1979, cited by Coke, 1991). In addition, several researchers have provided direct evidence that black grandparents are much more active and involved with their grandchildren than white grandparents (Cherlin & Furstenberg, 1986; Hentig, 1946; Pearson, Hunter, Ensminger, & Kellam, 1990).

While most of the literature concerned with the family role responsibilities of older blacks has focused on their role as grandparents, there are some data which indicate that older blacks perform a wide range of services that benefit various members of the extended family, whether they reside in a three-generation household or not. Coke (1991) interviewed male (N = 85) and female (N = 79) black elderly, and one of the questions she asked was, "What things do you do for family members?" Responses among males indicated that lending money was the most frequently mentioned service, mentioned by nearly 35 percent of respondents. This role was followed in order by doing chores (25.2 percent), cooking (16.5 percent), giving advice (13.0 percent), giving gifts (3.5 percent), baby-sitting (2.6 percent), visiting in hospital (2.6 percent), and motivating (1.7 percent). The list of services provided was rather similar among the elderly black women interviewed. The services mentioned by women included lending money (26.2 percent), giving advice (17.7 percent), doing chores (17.7 percent), cooking (17.0 percent), baby-sitting (9.2 percent), giving gifts (96.4 percent), visiting in hospital (3.5 percent), and providing a home (2.1 percent). Thus it is clear that the family role responsibilities of black elderly extend far beyond their roles as grandparents in three-generation households.

On the other hand, at least one study has yielded data suggesting that black and white elderly do not differ markedly with respect to the roles they play in the lives of their children and grandchildren. Mitchell and Register (1984) employed data from a national survey of Americans aged 65 and over to test a number of hypotheses based on the assumption that black elderly people are more likely than white elderly people to be part of an extended family. Specifically, the hypotheses they tested were that: (1) aged blacks see their children and grandchildren more often than aged whites; (2) aged blacks receive help from their children and grandchildren more often than aged whites; (3) aged blacks help their children and grandchildren more often than aged whites; and (4) aged blacks take grandchildren, nieces, or nephews into their homes to live with them more often than aged whites.

The sample included 334 blacks and 1,813 whites who had living children. The respondents ranged in age from 65 to 96 years. The median age among the whites was 72 years, and that for the blacks was 71 years. The two samples differed significantly with respect to annual income, educational level, and marital status. The whites had higher incomes. Only about 10 percent of the whites had annual incomes of less than $1,000, compared to 33 percent of the blacks. The educational differential between the black and white samples was comparable. Nearly 19 percent of the whites reported that they had completed high school, compared to less than four percent of the blacks. About half of the whites were married, and 46 percent were widowed. Only 39 percent of the blacks were married. Nearly 53 percent of the blacks were widowed. Mitchell and Register noted that these differences between the black and white samples were comparable to differences reported in other studies employing representative national samples.

The survey contained several groups of items designed to assess the research hypotheses. One item asked each respondent to indicate the last time he or she had seen his or her child(ren) and grandchild(ren). Response options for this question ranged from "live with them" through "longer than three months ago." A set of six items was used to measure the amount of help the respondents received from their children or grandchildren. These items were dichotomies. Respondents indicated whether or not they received each of the following categories of help: (1) care when someone is ill; (2) advice on running your home; (3) shop or run errands for you; (4) financial help; (5) advice on job or business matters; and (6) advice on how to deal with life's problems. A set of nine items measured the amount of help that respondents gave to their children or grandchildren. These items were also dichotomies. The categories of help included the following: (1) care when someone is ill; (2) advice on money matters; (3) shop or run errands for them; (4) help fix things around the house or keep house for them; (5) financial help; (6) take them places such as the doctor, shopping, or church; (7) advice on running their home; (8) advice on job or business matters; and (9) advice on how to deal with life's problems. Respondents were also asked to indicate whether they had ever taken children, grandchildren, nieces, or nephews into their home to live with them.

In comparing the black and white sample on these measures, Mitchell and Register controlled for socioeconomic status and area of residence. The measure of socioeconomic status that they used was the Hollingshead Index of Social Position. Area of residence was measured as a single item having four response categories: (1) rural, (2) town, (3) suburban, and (4) central city.

The findings indicated no significant difference between the black and white samples with respect to the last time that they had seen either their children or their grandchildren. Seventy-seven percent of the blacks and 81 percent of the whites had seen their children within the last two weeks. Seventy-three percent of the blacks and 74 percent of the whites reported that they had seen their grandchildren within the last two weeks. Thus hypothesis one was not confirmed. Mitchell and Register concluded that elderly blacks and elderly whites do not differ with respect to frequency of contact with their children and grandchildren.

In assessing the second and third hypotheses, Mitchell and Register calculated scale scores representing receiving and giving help. For each of these scores, a three-way analysis of variance was performed in which the independent variables were race (black versus white), socio-economic status (collapsed to low versus high) and area of residence (collapsed to rural versus urban). These analyses yielded a significant main effect due to race with respect to receiving help. The mean score for receiving help was significantly higher among the black elderly sample than among the elderly white sample. However, the analysis of scores for receiving help also yielded a significant race by socio-economic status interaction. The nature of this interaction was that among high socioeconomic status respondents the blacks reported receiving much more help than the whites, whereas among lower socioeconomic status respondents there was virtually no difference in the amount of help received. Thus it could be argued that there is no difference between the two races among those respondents who probably need help most, those of lower socioeconomic status. Furthermore, Mitchell and Register noted that race explained only a very small portion of the variability in receiving help, even among the low socioeconomic status respondents. The significance of the observed differences was due primarily to the large sample sizes employed in the study. Thus hypothesis two was confirmed, but the findings did not indicate very substantial differences between black and white elderly in terms of receiving help from their families.

Hypothesis 3, concerned with giving help to families, was not confirmed. The analysis of scale scores for giving help yielded neither a significant main effect due to race nor any significant two- or three-way interactions involving race. Thus Mitchell and Register concluded that elderly blacks and elderly whites do not in fact differ with respect to the amount of help that they provide to their families.

The fourth research hypothesis, concerned with taking children, grandchildren, nieces, and nephews into one's home, was confirmed. Nearly 32 percent of the blacks reported that they had taken children into their homes to live, compared to just 20 percent of the whites. This finding does support the notion that the black elderly are more heavily involved with family role responsibilities than elderly whites, and it could be interpreted as supporting the general view that the black elderly are more likely to be involved in extended family relationships. However, Mitchell and Register also pointed out that the magnitude of the observed difference was not great.

Thus the findings of Mitchell and Register (1984) provide only limited support for the theory that the black elderly are more likely to take on responsibilities with respect to children and grandchildren. They concluded that on balance their findings suggested that the stereotypical view of the involvement of the black elderly in extended family relationships was an unwarranted overgeneralization. They also suggested that the mediating effect of socioeconomic status on the family involvement variables implied that a more productive area for research would be the examination of differences between black and white elderly in terms of financial need. On balance, however, the literature does contain more studies supporting the view that black old people and more likely than white old people to be involved in extended family roles.

## FAMILY ROLE RESPONSIBILITIES
## AND LIFE SATISFACTION AMONG BLACK ELDERLY

There is both theoretical and empirical evidence that the family role responsibilities of elderly blacks are correlated positively with life satisfaction. Of course, traditional role theory suggests that for all people satisfaction with life is derived in part from the perception that one is performing useful roles (Rosow, 1967, 1973). According to Rosow (1973), the most crucial challenge of growing old is "the progressive loss of roles and functions of the aged, for this change represents a critical introduction of stress" that precipitates a profound existential crisis (p. 82). Rosow explained several aspects of the role loss experienced by the aged in our society that are stress inducing.

First, the loss of significant roles excludes older individuals from social participation and in so doing devalues them as individuals. The loss of valued roles in society may lead to a loss of self-esteem and self-worth. Although older individuals may still have much ability, our society places greater emphasis on economic utility, and the elderly are often viewed as marginal members of society. First, they are excluded from the mainstream, and then they are devalued because they no longer contribute. This devaluation is reflected in the tendency for older individuals to be patronized, ignored, or rejected as liabilities.

Second, role loss accounts for the stress-inducing reality that old age is generally associated with significant loss of status. Rosow pointed out that all previous developmental phases of life, including childhood, adolescence, and adulthood, are marked by steady gains in social status. Adolescents have more privileges and responsibilities than children, and adults more than adolescents. Throughout the successive milestones of adulthood status tends to increase. Education confers status, as does marriage, occupational selection and advancement, and parenthood. Each of these transitions is associated with increases in perceived competence, rewards, privileges, authority, and prestige. The status loss associated with old age represents a reversal of this lifelong trend toward increasing respect. In old age, the personal accomplishments of a lifetime tend to be overlooked. Individuality is lost, and one becomes a faceless member of a devalued class.

Third, Rosow (1973) argued that role loss is particularly troubling because individuals in American society are not socialized or prepared for the changes associated with aging. All other life transitions involve systematic preparation. Many transitions are marked by elaborate rites of passage that clearly delineate future roles and expectations. However, the role losses associated with old age are not accompanied by any socialization process. Therefore older individuals must adapt to their new status without the benefit of clear expectations or standards. Thus the stresses associated with role loss are compounded by the stress associated with uncertainty.

Fourth, Rosow noted that the loss of roles among the aged results in unstructured lives. In the absence of duties, the elderly are often without the benefit of normative expectations upon which they can structure their lives. While some older individuals are imaginative and creative enough to generate meaningful activities, many are not. Those who are not tend to experience boredom and depression.

Finally, Rosow concluded that the role loss associated with old age results in the loss of social identity. Since individuals tend to define themselves in terms of their social roles, the loss of roles translates into "a direct, sustained attack on the ego. If the social self consists of roles, then role loss erodes self-conceptions and sacrifices social identity" (p. 83).

The stressful nature of these aspects of role loss is manifested in a variety of negative outcomes. Rosow noted that older individuals have higher rates of mental illness and higher suicide rates than any other age group.

Of course, role theory would also strongly suggest that older individuals who do maintain significant social roles are more likely than those who do not, and this premise would in turn suggest that the black elderly, who we have seen tend to continue to perform significant roles within the family, might achieve a more balanced adjustment to old age than individuals from other cultural groups who may be less likely to continue to perform such roles. This contention would be consistent with the results of several studies indicating that even though elderly black Americans tend to be poorer and less healthy than elderly whites, the blacks typically score higher than whites on measures of life satisfaction and subjective well-being (Clavon & Smith, 1986; Morrisson, 1982).

Several empirical studies have provided data suggesting that involvement in significant roles within the family and extended family is indeed related to life satisfaction among black elderly. Farakhan, Lubin, and O'Connor (1984) studied the correlates of life satisfaction among a sample of 30 black Americans who ranged in age from 52 to 97 (mean + 71.4 years). All the research participants were retired. These respondents had a mean educational level of 9.2 years, and most had been employed as semi-skilled or skilled laborers. These respondents were each interviewed three times, with approximately one month between the interviews. The three interviews focused, respectively, on (1) the pre-retirement phase of their lives; (2) the immediate post-retirement phase; and (3) their immediate situation. The investigators measured psychological adjustment and life satisfaction using the Ecosystem Assessment Record (O'Connor, Klassen, & O'Conner, 1979). This measure assessed satisfaction with family, friends, social activities, work, health, education, as well as the amount of time devoted to each of these areas. Mood at the time of each interview was assessed using the Depression Adjective Check List-Form E (Lubin, 1981).

Farakhan and her associates found that the respondents indicated generally high levels of satisfaction in all of the areas that were assessed. However, over the three time intervals assessed, satisfaction in most areas decreased, while satisfaction with family increased. In the pre-retirement phase, work was the greatest source of satisfaction. In the immediate situation interview, family was the greatest source of satisfaction. Results also indicated a significant negative correlation between overall life satisfaction and time devoted to family and children. These data suggest that continued participation in family roles is a source of subjective well-being among black elderly.

Davidson and Cotter (1984) studied the relationships between the subjective well-being of elderly black and white adults and the extensiveness of their social networks at various levels, including family, neighbors, friendships, and membership in formal, organized groups. Subjective well-being was assessed by means of the OARS Multidimensional Functional Assessment Questionnaire (Pfeiffer, 1976). Nine items from this instrument were selected concerned with such psychological dimensions as life satisfaction, loneliness, happiness, anxiety, and enthusiasm. Social networks were measured by self-reports of frequency of contact. The investigators also assessed the extent to which respondents identified with the community in which they lived. The sample for the study consisted of 100 elderly blacks and 200 elderly whites from Tuscaloosa, Alabama, and Aiken, South Carolina.

The results of the study indicated that the black and white samples did not differ significantly with respect to overall life satisfaction. However, the elderly blacks scored significantly higher than the elderly whites on measures of social networks in the form of both family and organized groups. In contrast, elderly whites tended to score higher than elderly blacks on the measure of community identification. These findings suggest that family roles may be more important as a source of subjective well-being among black elderly than among white elderly.

Mutran (1985) also compared black and white elderly with respect to the relationship between subjective well-being and involvement in family and extended family roles. She concluded that black elderly are more likely than white elderly to both provide various forms of support to family members and to receive various forms of support from family members. She concluded that the extended family is much more important to the subjective well-being of elderly blacks than that of elderly whites. Mutran also reported that elderly adults who provide the most assistance to their family members tend to express the feeling that older adults deserve respect. Furthermore, these individuals were also more likely than other elderly respondents to indicate that their families actually did show them such respect. These findings provide direct support for Rosow's (1967, 1973) role theory.

Taylor (1985) used the data from the National Survey of African-Americans, conducted during 1979 and 1980, to investigate the role of the extended family as a source of support for black elderly. He reported that most blacks over the age of 55 tend to live with or in close proximity to extended family members, and they tend to have frequent contact with these family members. Taylor observed that the black elderly are among the most severely disadvantaged groups in American society, and that socioeconomic status is characteristically the strongest predictor of subjective well-being. Nevertheless, the black elderly in the National Survey demonstrated relatively high levels of subjective well-being. Taylor concluded that the support derived from frequent contact with family members may result in the relatively high levels of life satisfaction observed in the sample. However, Taylor did not directly test the hypothesis that there is a positive correlation between family role responsibilities and subjective well-being among the population of black elderly.

Coke (1991) did test this hypothesis directly. She asked her sample of 166 elderly black to list all their family members and to indicate, for each family member listed: (1) the number of hours per month of personal contact with the family member; (2) the number of hours of telephone contact; (3) the respondent's perception of how close he or she felt to the family member; (4) the number of activities carried out with the family member; (5) the services provided by the respondent to the family member; and

(6) the services provided to the respondent by the family member. Based on responses to these questions, Coke developed an index of family role involvement comprised of the total number of family members listed, the total number of activities reported across all the family members listed, the total number of services performed for all the family members listed, and the self-reported number of hours of face-to-face contact with the family members. Coke found a significant positive relationship for her total sample between scores on this index of family role involvement and scores on Diener's (1984) Subjective Well-Being Scale ($r = .36$, $p < .001$). Within-sex analyses indicated that the relationship between family role involvement and life satisfaction was significant for males ($r = .27$, $p < .01$), but not for females ($r = .18$, $p < .05$). This finding is attributable to the fact that the women in the sample were more homogeneous than the males, demonstrating generally high scores on both family role involvement and subjective well-being.

Additional support for the hypothesis that family role responsibilities are related to life satisfaction among the black elderly is provided by a naturalistic study described by Huling (1978). He presented a series of case studies of elderly black Americans and their relationships with their multigenerational families. These cases make it quite clear that the elderly members of the families derived great satisfaction from their interactions with their families. Huling concluded that elderly blacks have traditionally bolstered the cohesiveness of the family through the material, emotional, and spiritual support they provided for their children and grandchildren.

Huling's descriptions of the family roles assumed by black elderly make clear the connection to West African cultural traditions. He described grandparents passing on history and folklore, healing injuries and sicknesses, providing emotional support and spiritual counsel, transmitting important cultural values, and teaching critical survival skills. However, Huling also cautioned that these roles may be in jeopardy today, due to increased urbanization, upward social mobility, and the emergence of the nuclear family in contemporary black America. As younger black adults are forced to move in order to pursue their careers, the proportion of multigenerational households may decrease, limiting the involvement of grandparents with their children and grandchildren. In addition, Huling cited a trend for younger black adults to exercise more authority and to take greater responsibility for the upbringing of children, which might limit the influence of grandparents.

Of course, Huling's case study was reported 15 years ago, and the many more recent empirical studies of the black elderly have not suggested any diminution in their family role responsibilities. On the other hand, his caveats regarding the impact of continuing social and economic change within the black community would appear to justify continuing study in this area.

# Chapter 4

# The Church

## *HISTORICAL BACKGROUND*

Quarles (1987) made it clear that religion has been an important element in the lives of American blacks from the first days of slavery. Religion was deeply rooted in the African past. In the agrarian society of West Africa, the gods were associated closely with the land. There was one supreme deity and there were many lesser gods. The lesser gods were linked with various natural events and forces such as the sun, rivers, and winds. These gods had diviners who interpreted their will and attempted to predict the crops. Quarles noted that the West Africans also had numerous lesser spirits and deities who represented ancestors. These spirits were thought to reside in objects within the home and fields. The association of lesser deities with specific objects helps to explain the high level of development of African art in the form of masks and statues. Music and dance were also employed in the service of religion. For example, fertility dances were tantamount to prayers to the gods for a bountiful harvest.

During the era of slavery in America there were all-slave churches with slaves serving as pastors. However, some whites would always attend these services to make certain that nothing untoward took place. In fact, religion was used as a means of inculcating in slaves the belief that it was God's will that whites should rule and that slaves should be slaves. Quarles (1987) quoted a catechism that was written for the religious instruction of slaves:

> Question:    Who gave you a master and a mistress?
> Answer:      God gave them to me.
> Question:    Who says that you must obey them?
> Answer:      God says that I must.

(p. 71)

The sermons and hymns in these slave churches could not deal directly with issues of social injustice that concerned the system of slavery. Instead, the worship tended to focus on other-worldly topics, like the beauties of heaven. Quarles argued that slaves did find an outlet for their frustrations in some of the spirituals they sang, which had double meanings. For example, the spiritual "Go Down, Moses" refers to Egypt and implores Moses to tell Pharaoh to let my people go. Similarly, Quarles quoted the autobiography of a former slave as suggesting that in the hymn "O Canaan, Sweet Canaan" the land of Canaan was in fact a reference to the North, to which the slaves yearned to escape. Thus the spirituals sung by slaves did provide somewhat of a vehicle for protest, although clearly in a disguised form.

The church was also important among free blacks in the North during the antebellum period. Most blacks in the North were members of all-Negro congregations. This was the direct result of discrimination against blacks in other churches. Blacks in white churches were typically required to sit in designated pews and to wait to take communion until all the whites had done so. The first independent black church was founded in Philadelphia in 1794 by Richard Allen who had been angered when he was asked to sit at the rear of the gallery of St. George's Methodist Episcopal Church. This church was initially affiliated with the Methodist organization of the United States, but as the number of black churches grew the black Methodists severed their tie with the whites and established their own national organization. The same trend toward all-black congregations developed among Baptists around 1800.

It is important to note that these all-black churches did not develop because of any difference with respect to religious doctrine. The impetus was purely social and political in nature. The blacks wanted to have control over their own church and to be free from discrimination. It is not surprising, therefore, that these black churches in the North should be involved in various social and political activities. When the churches existed in towns where black children were banned from attending the public schools, the church hall was often used as a school, with church elders serving as the teachers. Black churches also became meeting places for abolitionist groups, and some black churches were stops on the underground railroad.

By the advent of the twentieth century, the black churches had become powerful institutions. The church served as a community center and a social welfare agency. Black churches were instrumental in the founding of many institutions of higher education that provided higher education to thousands of students.

## THE BLACK CHURCH IN AMERICA TODAY

Billingsley (1992) noted that "the black church is at the leading edge of the African-American community's push to influence the future of its families" (p. 349). Billingsley offered several reasons for the importance of the black church, not the least of which is the fact that religious orientation is "one of the greatest historic strengths of black families."

Billingsley, Caldwell, Hill, and Rouse (1991) have estimated that there are nearly 76,000 black churches in the United States, and Lincoln and Mamiya (1990) estimated that there were nearly 24 million members of black churches in 1989. Nearly half of these church members were affiliated with one of the three large Baptist denominations, the National Baptist Convention, U.S.A., the National Baptist Convention of America, and the Progressive National Baptist Convention. An additional 18 percent of these church members are affiliated with one of the three major black Methodist denominations, the African Methodist Episcopal, the African Methodist Episcopal Zion, and the Christian Methodist Episcopal church.

Billingsley (1992) emphasized the role of the black church as "a preserver of the African-American heritage and an agent for reform" (p. 350). He argued that in fact no successful movement for improving the conditions of life of African-Americans has occurred without the support of the church.

But it should not be concluded that black church members are more concerned with political and social reform than they are with religion itself. Billingsley (1992) reported the results of a secondary analysis of the data from the National Survey of Black Americans which clearly indicated the value placed by black Americans on religious faith. This analysis indicated that 84 percent of black adults considered themselves to be religious individuals. Eighty percent of the adults surveyed felt that it is very important to send one's children to church. Seventy-six percent of the sample indicated that religion is very important when one is young, and 76 percent of the sample indicated that religion is very important in their lives currently. Within the sample of the National Survey of Black Americans, 78 percent of the sample reported that they pray daily, and 71 percent indicated that they attend church regularly (at least once a month).

Data relevant to the religious practices of the black elderly was made available by Coke (1991) based on her survey of 166 elderly blacks in the New York area. She reported that 62 percent of her sample attended church on a weekly basis, including 48 percent of the males and 77 percent of the females. Coke also asked her informants to indicate the extent to which they agreed with the statement, "I am a religious individual." Figure 4.1 presents the distribution of responses to this item among the males and females in Coke's sample. The data in the figure indicate that 86.1 percent of the female respondents and 42.6

Figure 4.1. Frequency Distributions of Responses to the Statement, "I Am a Religious Individual" Among Male and Female Respondents to Coke's (1991) Survey of Elderly Blacks

| RESPONSE | MALES | | FEMALES | |
|---|---|---|---|---|
| | N | % | N | % |
| Strongly Disagree | 5 | 5.7 | 5 | 6.3 |
| Disagree | 12 | 13.8 | 2 | 2.5 |
| Neither Agree Nor Disagree | 33 | 37.9 | 4 | 5.1 |
| Agree | 24 | 27.7 | 21 | 26.6 |
| Strongly Agree | 13 | 14.9 | 47 | 59.5 |

percent of the male respondents indicated agreement with this statement. This finding is in accord with the findings reported by Billingsley for the black population in general, which also suggested that women were more likely than men to view themselves as religious individuals.

## RELIGION AND LIFE SATISFACTION

There is evidence that religion is a predictor of life satisfaction among both the general population of older individuals and the black elderly. With respect to the general population, several empirical investigations have demonstrated positive correlations between measures of church attendance and self-rated religiosity and measures of life satisfaction or subjective well-being (Blazer & Palmore, 1976; Hadaway, 1978; Gray & Moberg, 1977). At least one report (Steinitz, 1980) disputed this association, reporting no consistent relationship between measures of religious participation and measures of well-being. However, the latter study appears to have employed particularly specific measures of religiosity that may lack general applicability. These included measures of strength of affiliation with a particular religious denomination, confidence in the relevance of organized religious activity, and strength of one's belief in life after death.

A study reported by Hunsberger (1985) appears to be a methodologically sound effort to determine the relationship between religious participation and life satisfaction. Hunsberger interviewed 33 men and 52 women between the ages of 65 and 88. The respondents were residents of apartments for the elderly in Ontario, Canada. The interview included a number of measures of religious participation and belief, including: (1) a 24-item scale measuring the orthodoxy of their religious beliefs ( the Christian Orthodoxy Scale; Fullerton & Hunsberger, 1982); (2) a measure of the amount of emphasis that had been placed on religion during the respondent's childhood; (3) a measure of the extent to which the respondent agrees with the religious beliefs that he or she was taught; (4) a measure of the respondent's perception of the importance of religious beliefs; and (5) a self-report measure of frequency of church attendance. The interview also included four different measures of life satisfaction, including self-rated happiness, adjustment, satisfaction with health, and the degree to which one perceives one's life as exciting.

The results of the study were as follows: Self-rated happiness was correlated significantly ($p < .05$) with all five of the measures of religiosity. It was correlated most strongly with the extent to which the individual agreed with the religious beliefs that he or she had been taught ($r = .45$, $p < .001$). It was correlated next most strongly with the importance the individual ascribed to those beliefs ($r = .30$, $p < .01$). Self-rated adjustment was also correlated significantly ($p < .05$ ) with all five measures of religiosity. Adjustment was also correlated most strongly with the degree to which the respondent agreed with the beliefs that he or she had been taught ($r = .31$, $p < .01$). Satisfaction with one's health was correlated significantly with two of the five measures of religiosity: (1) the respondent's perception of the emphasis on religion during childhood ($r = .20$, $p < .05$), and (2) the importance the respondent ascribed to religious beliefs ($r = .25$, $p < .01$). Finally, the extent to which the respondent perceived his or her life as exciting was correlated significantly with three of the measures of religiosity: (1) the emphasis placed on religion during the respondent's childhood ($r = .29$, $p < .01$); (2) the respondent's perception of the importance of religious beliefs ($r = .26$, $p < .01$); and (3) self-reported church attendance ($r = .22$, $p < .05$). These results provide broad support for the notion that religiosity is related to life satisfaction and subjective well-being.

There is also empirical evidence of a correlation between religious activity and life satisfaction among the black elderly specifically. In the study referred to above, Coke (1991) reported that among her pooled sample of male and female senior citizens, there was a significant positive correlation between hours per week of participation in church activities and scores on the Diener Satisfaction with Life Scale ($r = .22$, $p < .01$). Thus there is not only evidence that religion is important to elderly blacks, but also evidence that religious activity is positively associated with subjective well-being. Additional data relevant to the question of the relationship between religious activity and life satisfaction is presented in the section on empirical research that follows.

## EMPIRICAL STUDIES OF THE ROLE OF RELIGION IN THE LIVES OF ELDERLY BLACKS

There is a substantial body of empirical research which suggests that participation in church activity and self-rated religiosity are related positively to the life satisfaction of elderly blacks. The historical role of the black church in providing social welfare services to the black community has provided church members with extensive opportunities for involvement in social service activities. These activities have been particularly important for elderly church members, since they enable older persons to remain involved in the community (Carter, 1982; Taylor, Thornton, & Chatters, 1987). In addition, these activities allow black seniors to develop networks of friends to whom they can turn for emotional or tangible support when necessary (Hines & Boyd-Franklin, 1982; Taylor & Chatters, 1986). Steinitz (1980) reported that churches provide both tangible assistance and psychological support for elderly blacks and whites. She concluded that the role of the church was particularly crucial for elderly members who do not have families living near them.

Walls and Zarit (1991) provided a detailed description of the perceptions of older blacks regarding the amount and type of support they receive from their church. The investigators interviewed 98 elderly black church members who were residing in an urban community in central Pennsylvania. They measured perceived social support received from family and church, as well as self-rated religiosity, well-being, health status, and functional ability. They also measured the respondents' social networks, using the SS-R (Vaux & Harrison, 1985). This procedure asks respondents to list up to 15 people to whom they feel close. For each individual nominated, the respondent also indicated the type of relationship, frequency of interaction, and whether or not the individual was a fellow church member.

Walls and Zarit (1991) found that 40 percent of the individuals who were named as close associates of the respondents were members of the respondents' churches. Fifty percent of those nominated were members of the respondents' families. The respondents reported participating in a wide variety of church-related activities. Some of these were spiritual in nature, including worship services, pastoral visits, and bible classes. Other activities mentioned were nonspiritual. These included social activities and trips, preventive health screenings, assistance with household and health problems, and transportation to church, doctors, and shopping.

The investigators regressed subjective well-being, measured

by the 17-item Philadelphia Geriatric Center (PGC) Morale Scale (Lawton, 1975), on self-rated religiosity, participation in church activities, perceived social support from families, and perceived social support from church. This analysis indicated that perceived overall support from church members was related significantly to well-being. The other predictors included in this analysis were not significant. Although the respondents reported receiving somewhat more social support from family and friends than from church members, the support that they received from the church members was related significantly to subjective well-being, while that received from family members was not. These findings are particularly interesting in view of the fact that all of the participants in this study were church members. Had individuals who were not church members been included in the sample and assigned a score of zero for support derived from church members, the relationship reported between well-being and support from church members might have been stronger. Other empirical investigations that have reported significant relationships between the subjective well-being of older blacks and the social networks associated with participation in church activities have been reported by Taylor and Chatters (1986), Ortega, Crutchfield, and Rushing (1983), and Krause and Tran (1989).

Taylor and Chatters (1991) provided some data suggesting that elderly black Americans are not only likely to be involved with church and church-related activities, but are also likely to engage in many private activities indicating the importance of religion. The sample used in this study was the National Survey of Black Americans (NSBA), a nationally representative sample of 2,107 black Americans over the age of 18. Of the total sample, 581 respondents were 55 years old or older. Within this subsample of older individuals Taylor and Chatters found that 43.9 percent of respondents reported reading religious books or materials every day, and another 23.9 percent reported reading such materials on a weekly basis. One-third of their older subsample reported that they watched or listened to TV or radio programs about religion on a daily basis, and another 50 percent indicated that they tuned in to such programs on a weekly basis. Thus more than 83 percent of the sample tuned in to religious programming frequently. Nearly 94 percent of this sample reported that they prayed on a daily basis, and nearly 80 percent reported that they asked others to pray for them.

These data make it clear that older black Americans tend to be a very religious group, and that their religiosity is not confined to the social aspect of church attendance. Unfortunately, Taylor and Chatters (1991) did not report correlations between these indicators of nonorganizational religious participation and the subjective well-being of the older adults in their sample. Some data relevant to the relationship between religiosity and subjective well-being is provided in the study by Coke (1991) noted earlier in this chapter. Coke did not measure specific nonorganizational religious behaviors, but she did assess self-rated religiosity and relate this variable to subjective well-being. Coke reported a correlation of .54 ($p < .001$) between religiosity and Diener's Satisfaction with Life Scale among male respondents, and a correlation of .38 ($p < .001$) between these variables among female respondents.

Thus it is clear that the church and religion have been and continue to be important aspects of the lives of elderly black Americans. It appears that both the social aspect of church membership and religious faith itself are significant contributors to the subjective well-being of this group.

## THE INTERACTION OF RELIGIOUS PARTICIPATION AND SOCIAL SUPPORT PATTERNS

A recent study by Hatch (1991) indicated that there is an interaction between religious participation and informal social support patterns among elderly black women, such that religious involvement is associated with greater utilization of social support and greater provision of social support. Hatch employed samples of 126 African-American women aged 60 and above and 1,313 white women aged 60 and above. These samples were drawn from the National Survey of Families and Households (NSFH), a national probability survey of 9,643 households in which one adult was selected at random from each household surveyed to complete the study.

The dependent variables employed in the study were six factor-based scales measuring: (1) reliance on one's children for help in an emergency, for financial assistance, or for advice; (2) reliance on nonrelatives for help under the same circumstances; (3) self-reported help actually received from children during the month preceding the survey in the areas of transportation, home or auto repairs, other work around the house, or emotional support; (4) self-reported help actually received from nonrelatives over the same period in the same areas; (5) self-reported help provided by the respondent to her children during the month preceding the survey; and (6) self-reported help provided by the respondent to nonrelatives during the same period. Hatch reported that these scales had good internal consistency reliabilities within both the black and white samples.

The predictors employed by Hatch included: (1) race; (2) family variables, including current marital status, number of times married, number of children, and number of persons living in the household; (3) paid work history; (4) religious participation variables, including frequency of attending religious services and frequency of attending church or synagogue social events; and (5) social interaction variables, including self-reports of the number of evenings per month the respondent spent with family members and the number of evenings per month the respondent spent with friends, neighbors, or co-workers. Hatch also included several additional measures as control variables. These were: (1) measures of health, including self-reported health limitations and self-perceived health compared to other individuals of the same age; (2) self-reported annual personal income and family income; (3) age; and (4) ownership of a motor vehicle.

Hatch analyzed her data by means of six hierarchical multiple regression analyses, one for each of the informal social support measures. In each of these analyses the control variables and the respondent background and demographic characteristics were included at step one; the religious participation variables and the social interaction variables were included at step two; and a product term representing the interaction of race and attendance of religious social events was included at the final step. In this manner, the difference between black and white respondents with respect to the effect of religious social activity on each of the informal support variables was tested only after the effects of all the other predictors had been partialled out.

These analyses yielded significant race by religious social activity interactions for four of the six dependent variables. With respect to reliance on children for help, the significant interaction indicated that religious social activity was a more important predictor for black women than for white women, with more frequent attendance associated with lower likelihood of relying on children for help. With respect to reliance on nonrelatives for help, religious social activity was again a more important predictor for black women than for white women. In this case, however, the black women who attended religious social events more frequently were more likely to rely on nonrelatives for help than were women who attended less frequently.

Significant interactions were also obtained with respect to both self-reported help provided to children and self-reported help provided to nonrelatives during the month preceding the survey. With respect to help provided to children, attendance at religious social events was a more important predictor for black women than for white women. Those who attended religious social events more frequently tended to report less actual help to their children than those who attended religious social events less frequently. With respect to help provided to nonrelatives, attendance at religious social events was also a more important predictor for blacks than for whites. Those women who attended more religious social events tended to report that they had provided more such help than those who attended fewer religious social events.

Based on Hatch's study, it would appear that blacks and whites differ in the relationship between participation in religious social activities and patterns of informal support. Given the literature suggesting that life satisfaction is related to participation in family roles and to the availability of social support, these findings lead one to suspect that among the black elderly the effects of religiosity on life satisfaction may be both direct and indirect. Thus elderly blacks appear to: (1) derive satisfaction directly from their religious faith; (2) benefit directly from the social interaction associated with church membership; and (3) benefit indirectly from the social interactions that are associated with church-related social events.

# Chapter 5

# A Model for Predicting Life Satisfaction Among the Black Elderly

The literature reviewed in the foregoing chapters makes it clear that a model designed for the prediction of life satisfaction among the black elderly must include sociodemographic factors as well as variables tapping the domains of family roles, participation in church-related activities, and self-perceptions of personal religiosity. It also appears that both objective measures (e.g., perceived adequacy of income) must be included in the model.

The anthropological literature clearly suggests that the black elderly enjoy a different status within the family and extended family than do the white elderly. The literature on the black churches of America and the importance of religion to black Americans similarly suggests that these areas are of much greater importance to older blacks than to older whites. However, the literature on the black elderly contains relatively little work pertinent to the issue of the relative contributions to life satisfaction of family role responsibilities, church participation, religiosity, and sociodemographic indicators. Accordingly, it was pertinent to develop a multivariate model that incorporates all these domains. The model developed for this purpose is depicted graphically in Figure 5.1. In this chapter, the model is explicated, and operational definitions for the predictor variables and the dependent variable are provided.

Figure 5.1. Multidimensional Model for the Prediction of Life Satisfaction Among Elderly Black Americans

| Predictors | | Dependent Variable |
|---|---|---|
| Domain | Variable | |
| Objective Socio-Demographic Indicators | Gender | Life Satisfaction |
| | Age | |
| | Actual Income | |
| | Occupational Level | |
| | Educational Level | |
| Subjective (Self-Perception) Indicators | Health Status | |
| | Adequacy of Income | |
| The Family | Current Family Role Responsibilities | |
| Church and Religion | Church Membership | |
| | Hours of Weekly Participation in Church Activities | |
| | Self-Perceived Religiosity | |

## INDEPENDENT (PREDICTOR) VARIABLES

### Gender

The traditional roles of women and men in West African society, the roles of male and female slaves, and the roles of contemporary black men and women in family, church, and society have been quite different. It was not expected that the factors which predicted life satisfaction among elderly black women would be the same as those which predicted life satisfaction among elderly black men. Gender was included in the model in order to compare women and men on both life satisfaction and the other independent variables. It was anticipated that when the model was tested, empirically significant gender differences would be found, and the separate prediction equations would have to be developed for each gender group.

## Age

Several studies have suggested that social role participation declines steadily with advancing age. Therefore the possible relationships between age and both role participation and life satisfaction should be assessed, in the event that chronological age must be controlled statistically in evaluating the contributions of the remaining predictors to the estimation of life satisfaction. Age is measured through self-report of a respondent's date of birth, which is transformed to age in years during analysis of data. This minimizes any tendency a respondent may have to prevaricate about his or her age.

## Income

Socioeconomic status has been shown to be an important predictor of subjective well-being among individuals of all ages from diverse cultural groups. Usui, Keil, and Durig (1985) interviewed 704 persons over the age of 60, many of whom were African-Americans. They found that the individual's financial status, relative to other elderly persons in their geographic area, was positively related to life satisfaction. They found that life satisfaction was highest when the seniors were better off financially than their closest relatives, and their children. According to the authors, in American society people expect that their children will be better off financially than they are themselves. If, in fact, the parent is more sound financially than the offspring, this situation may heighten his or her sense of "well-being," because he/she has fared better than expected.

On a more pragmatic level, one's actual annual income would be expected to be related to life satisfaction because a higher income would make it possible to purchase life's necessities and luxuries. A higher income can also lead to a better diet and to more regular access to health care, which might also be reflected in one's life satisfaction.

It has been noted that even though older African-Americans are typically poorer than older whites, older African-Americans typically score higher than older whites on measures of life satisfaction (Clavon & Smith, 1986; Morrisson, 1982). This suggests that among African-Americans there may be other factors that contribute to life satisfaction. However, these data should not be construed as obviating the importance of money to older blacks. Actual income was ascertained through respondent self-report.

### Occupational Level

Occupational level is an important component of socioeconomic status that could impact on the life satisfaction of an older person in a variety of ways, even after the individual has retired. Role theory (Rosow, 1973) suggests that individuals derive significant satisfaction and self-esteem from the roles they perform. Retirement may be experienced as stressful due to the loss of work roles. This loss might well be more severe among individuals who held professional or managerial jobs during their careers than among individuals with more menial jobs, due to the status associated with higher level occupations. Thus older blacks who had higher level jobs over the course of their lifetimes might manifest lower satisfaction with life following retirement. On the other hand, individuals who had held higher level jobs might have developed more effective coping techniques and more extensive support networks than individuals who held lower level jobs. These factors could result in higher levels of life satisfaction among individuals with higher occupational levels.

Occupational level is assessed by asking respondents to indicate the job they held during the greatest portion of their careers.

Responses are recorded and coded for occupational level subsequently. Responses are coded as representing blue collar, white collar, or professional occupations. Finer classifications, such as that embodied in the Hollinshead two-factor index of socioeconomic status, could not be made reliably based on the participants' responses.

## Educational Level

One's level of education is another important component of socioeconomic status that may be related directly to life satisfaction or may be related to life satisfaction indirectly through church involvement, financial satisfaction, or perceived health status. Individuals with higher levels of educational attainment might have interests that are less heavily affected by the aging process than the interests of less well-educated individuals. Educational level is assessed through the respondents' self-reports of the number of years of education completed.

## Health Status

Previous research conducted on the general population over 65 has suggested that the two strongest correlates of life satisfaction are perceived health condition and adequacy of income (Edwards & Klemmack, 1973; Spreitzer & Snyder, 1974). Several studies have indicated that subjective estimates of one's health status are related to subjective well-being (Liang, 1986; Gunter & Kolanowski, 1986; Weinberger, Darnell, Martz, Hiner, Neil, & Tierney, 1986).

Liang referred to the subjective health model as representing the individual's health in terms of the individual's self-perception, representing various aspects of health in a single summary rating. Liang tied these three models together when he commented that a person's objective health status affects his role performance. According to Liang, one's subjective self-reported health status derives from both one's objective physical condition and one's perception of the adequacy of one's role performance. Liang's conceptualization is particularly relevant to the question raised in the first chapter of this book, i.e., why is it that elderly African-Americans, whose health is objectively poorer than that of their white counterparts, nevertheless indicate comparable levels of life satisfaction. If elderly African-Americans tend to continue to fill important roles in their extended families, these roles may serve to bolster the individual's sense of efficacy and even the individual's view of his or her health status.

Health status is assessed in terms of the respondent's self-report on a single-item global health self-rating scale that requires the respondent to indicate whether his health is poor, fair, good, or excellent.

### Adequacy of Income

As suggested by the research of Usui, Keil, and Durig (1985), income has both absolute and relative significance. One's actual income is important, but so is one's income relative to that of other individuals who are available for comparison. Further, different individuals have different lifestyles requiring different amounts of money. Thus an income level that would be perceived as inadequate by one individual might be perceived as perfectly adequate by another.

Adequacy of income is assessed by a single self-report item asking respondents to indicate whether they perceive their income to be "not adequate," "more or less adequate," or "adequate."

### Current Family Role Responsibilities

In his description of role theory, Rosow (1973) suggested that satisfaction with life is in part a function of the sense of self-efficacy and self-esteem which is derived from the fulfillment of those social works which are perceived as important. Rosow noted that older persons in general must face the loss of previously held roles. They are no longer breadwinners or homemakers as they once were. They find themselves for the first time suffering a loss of status as a group. With each succeeding life period from childhood, through adolescence and adulthood, there was a corresponding increase in their status in the society. With old age this reverses for the first time, even though there has been no personal failure to warrant it.

Old age in America is not a state that we are socialized to accept or regard with anticipation. Older people are not prepared for the abrupt and radical changes in their lifestyles. Their responsibilities may become minimal. Deprived of any structure or obligations, they have no definite role to play in the society and are indeed subject to feeling useless and superfluous.

In the face of these feelings, older people become subject to a new type of stress. Not only are these people now in a position to have to deal with negative social implications of growing old, but they may experience physical incapacities or lose the ability to perform once manageable tasks. They may also face such crisis situations as the loss of a mate. Older persons demonstrate considerable variability in their adaption to such stresses.

Rosow pointed out that existing research shows that people can withstand stress effectively if there is a good strong support system to assist people in times of travail. Old people tend to show a major reduction in group memberships and the weakening of buffers against stress derived from residential changes, deaths of loved ones, declining health, and lower income. These detrimental effects could be moderated by continued role responsibilities within the structure of the family. As noted above, the African heritage of oral transmission of history has led to an honored social status for the elderly, and Wylie (1971) stressed that this tradition was not disrupted by slavery.

Several research studies have indicated that the African-American elderly tend to have more extensive involvement than their white counterparts with their families, extended families, and community. Rubenstein (1972) studied the social participation of African-American and white elderly. He found that elderly African-Americans were less likely than whites to live alone or with a spouse only. They were more likely than whites to live in an intergenerational household. Linn and Hunter (1979) surveyed African American, white, and Cuban elderly in the Miami area. They confirmed Rubenstein's finding that African-Americans were more likely than whites to reside in multigenerational households. Although these authors did not relate residence in an extended family household to subjective well-being or morale, they did note that psychosocial support is one of the functions typically attributed to the extended family system. They speculated that "in view of the various losses that accompany old age, such support could be invaluable in terms of self-esteem." Linn and her associates also noted that the African-Americans in their sample manifested the highest level of life satisfaction of any of the three ethnic groups included in the study.

Huling (1978) described a series of case studies of older African-Americans and their relationships with their multigenerational families. In these cases it was clear that the elderly members of the families derived great satisfaction from their roles as responsible family members. Huling concluded that "historically, older African Americans have provided a cohesiveness for the family by offering both material and spiritual support to their children and grandchildren" (p. 287). Huling described the roles of the older African-American family members as including passing on family history and folklore, healing injuries and sickness, providing advice and counsel, transmitting values, and teaching important survival skills. Huling also warned that these roles may be in jeopardy today, due to urbanization and the increased mobility of younger African-Americans. Huling also noted that younger African-American parents are "exercising more authority and assuming more responsibility for the up-bringing of their children, which curtails the amount of influence that grandparents have over grandchildren" (p. 288). Thus another reason for investigating the relationship between family role responsibility and life satisfaction among the African-American elderly is that these roles may well be undergoing a period of change at the present time.

Family role responsibilities are assessed by asking respondents to name all the family members with whom they have a current relationship. It is not required that the relatives named reside in the same home. For each family member nominated, the respondent is asked to name all the activities performed on a regular basis with that family member, as well as all the services the respondent performs for that family members (e.g., cooking, baby-sitting, advice, etc.) on a regular basis. Each respondent receives a score for family role responsibility equal to the number of activities and services listed, across all nominated family members.

### *Church and Religion*

The literature reviewed indicated clearly that the church is important to elderly black Americans, because of the network of social affiliation and support that the church provides, and because black Americans tend to be deeply religious. Thus Lindsay and Hawkins (1974) reported that elderly African-Americans received a great deal of informal and formal support from their churches. Thus also Taylor and Chatters (1986) reported that church-based informal support was very important among African-Americans in the United States over the age of 55, and they noted that church supports tended to become relatively more important as family supports declined. Smith (1986) studied the relationships between church attendance and morale among Southern African-Americans 55 years and older. She found that those who participated in church activities generally reported that they were "better off" than those who did not. She also noted that the churches that "ascribed status based on the criterion of advance age" attracted as many people who were "worse off" as it did those who were "better off." One of the interesting aspects of church activity is that a given member might on one occasion act to provide support and assistance to a fellow church or community member, and on another occasion receive assistance. For example, a "young-old" senior citizen might devote much time to providing transportation to older church members who need it, and on another occasion he might benefit from a pastoral visit during a hospital stay. Thus it would appear that a measure of involvement in church activities should include all participation, rather than the provision of specific services.

Church involvement is assessed in terms of (1) church membership, and (2) the average number of hours per week of church-related activities, including church attendance, community service activities, and social activities.

Taylor and Chatters (1991) made it clear that elderly blacks engaged in a large number of religious activities that are not related directly to church membership or participation in church activities. These activities include reading religious materials, tuning in to religious TV or radio broadcasts, and prayer. It therefore seemed essential to include as a predictor of life satisfaction a measure of religiosity independent of church membership and church-related activities. It was considered important that this measure capture the respondent's subjective self-perception, so an item was adopted from a prior study by Coke (1991) that requested the respondent to indicate the extent to which he or she agreed with the statement, "I am a religious individual." This question is asked orally while showing the respondent a card showing five response options ranging from "strongly disagree" to "strongly agree." The respondent could then indicate his or her response orally or by pointing to the desired response.

## DEPENDENT VARIABLE

The dependent variable, life satisfaction, was defined operationally by scores on the Diener Satisfaction with Life Scale (Diener, 1984; Diener, Emmons, Larsen, & Griffin, 1985). This is a measure of global life satisfaction or subjective well-being. It is ideal for use with older populations and in research situations where time of administration is an important factor, because the scale contains only five items. These items are presented in Figure 5.2. The scale is typically administered using a seven-point Likert-type response format, with response options ranging from "strongly disagree" to "strongly agree." For ease of administration, this was modified to a five-point Likert-type format with the same poles.

Diener and his associates (1986) normed their scale on several large undergraduate samples. Their data indicated that the scale was internally consistent, as indicated by item-total correlations ranging from .57 to .75 for the five items. Diener did not report an internal consistency reliability coefficient for the scale, but

Figure 5.2. The Five Items of the Diener Satisfaction with Life Scale, with Factor Loadings and Item-Total Correlations Reported by Diener et al. (1986)

|  | Factor Loading | Item-Total Correlation |
|---|---|---|
| 1. In most ways my life is close to my ideal. | .84 | .75 |
| 2. The conditions of my life are excellent. | .77 | .69 |
| 3. I am satisfied with my life. | .83 | .75 |
| 4. So far I have gotten the important things I want in life. | .72 | .67 |
| 5. If I could live my life over, I would change almost nothing. | .61 | .57 |

one may presume it would have been excellent on the basis of the item-total correlations. Coke (1989) did report an alpha coefficient of .87 for the five-item scale, based on a sample of 166 black elderly.

With respect to the validity of the SWLS, Diener and his associates (1986) reported significant positive correlations between scores on the scale and scores on nine other measures of subjective well-being. These correlations ranged from .50 to .75 and were all highly significant.

The SWLS was administered to seniors orally, with a card indicating the five response options for each question (strongly disagree, disagree, unsure, agree, strongly agree). Each statement was read aloud, after which respondents stated their response orally or pointed to the response on the card.

# Chapter 6

# An Empirical Investigation
# of Predictors of Life Satisfaction
# Among the Black Elderly

The foregoing chapters set forth a model for predicting life satisfaction among elderly blacks. Based on the literature concerned with life satisfaction among the general population of older individuals, it was hypothesized that self-perceived personal health and self-perceived adequacy of income would be significant predictors of life satisfaction. It was also expected that actual yearly household income, educational level, and occupational level would be related to life satisfaction in this population.

Based on the extensive literature on black culture, it was hypothesized further that involvement with one's family and with church activities would be strong predictors of life satisfaction among elderly black Americans.

This chapter presents the results of an empirical investigation carried out to test this model. A structured interview was administered to 144 elderly black males and 120 elderly black females who were recruited at 29 different senior citizens' centers in the greater New York area. Through this interview, the investigators assessed the predictors of life satisfaction included in the model, as well as self-reported life satisfaction.

The chapter has been organized under major headings corresponding to the methods and results of the study.

## METHODS

### Procedures

The study participants were recruited during site visits made by the authors and their assistants to senior citizen centers throughout the five boroughs of New York City. A total of 60 site visits by one or more investigators were required to complete the data collection.

On each visit participants were approached on a nonrandom convenience sampling basis. The investigators solicited the participation of any client who was present and not actively involved in some other activity at that time. Almost all the clients who were approached did agree to participate in the interview, once the investigator had explained the purpose of the study and had assured them that all their responses would be held strictly confidential.

It is recognized that the sampling procedure employed in this study limits the generalizability of the survey findings. Clearly, since all respondents were attending senior citizens' centers, the results of the study obviously cannot be generalized to invalids, to older persons residing in institutional settings, to individuals who choose not to attend. In addition, the results may be unique to the population of black senior citizens who reside in New York.

The interviews were administered in private offices made available to the investigators within the respective senior citizens' centers. These were typically the offices of the directors of the centers. The seniors who participated in the study were generally open and in fact eager to discuss their family roles and responsibilities in this setting.

### The Instrument

The study employed a structured interview format containing both forced choice and open-ended items. The instrument was designed to measure self-perceived health, self-perceived adequacy of income, actual yearly household income, the respondent's educational and occupational level, family role responsibility, and involvement in church-related activities. The interview also assessed life satisfaction.

The interview items measuring self-perceived health and self-perceived adequacy of income were taken from the instrument used by Spreitzer and Snyder (1974). Life satisfaction was assessed by the five-item scale developed and validated by Diener (1984).

Family role responsibility was measured as follows: Respondents were asked to list all of the family members with whom they had an ongoing relationship. The family members did not necessarily have to reside in the same home. Then the respondent was asked to indicate for each of these individuals the activities performed regularly with that person and the services provided regularly to that person. The number of activities and services mentioned was counted across all the family members nominated to obtain an overall family role involvement score.

In addition to interview items designed to assess life satisfaction and its predictors, the structured interview format included additional items to assess background and demographic factors including age, current employment status, and current living situation. The interview also contained a single question that asked respondents to rate themselves on the importance of religion in their lives.

The entire structured interview format was reviewed for content validity and clarity by two research specialists, one with a PhD in sociology and the other a PhD research psychologist. The instrument was revised based on their comments and was piloted on a group of three black seniors recruited at senior citizens centers. These pilot interviews confirmed that the questions were comprehensible and relevant to the participants. The pilot administrations also confirmed that the interview format required approximately one hour to complete. The three pilot participants were not included in the study sample.

# RESULTS

## Description of Sample

Table 6.1 presents the frequency distributions (for categorical variables) or descriptive statistics (for interval scale variables) for the background and demographic characteristics of the sample. The data in the table show that the sample contained 144 males (54.5 percent) and 120 females (45.5 percent). The majority of participants were retired (58.3 percent), and the majority reported having been employed in blue collar occupations. Half of the respondents reported that they were living with a spouse at

Table 6.1. Sample Background and Demographic Characteristics

| Variable | Value | N | % |
|----------|-------|---|---|
| Gender | Male | 144 | 54.5 |
|  | Female | 120 | 45.5 |
| Employment Status | Full Time | 34 | 12.9 |
|  | Part Time | 26 | 9.8 |
|  | Unemployed | 50 | 18.9 |
|  | Retired | 154 | 58.3 |
| Occupational Level | Professional | 8 | 3.0 |
|  | White Collar | 40 | 15.2 |
|  | Blue Collar | 216 | 81.8 |
| Living Situation | Alone | 60 | 22.7 |
|  | With Spouse | 132 | 50.0 |
|  | With Family | 48 | 18.2 |
|  | Non-Family | 24 | 9.1 |
| Church Member? | Yes | 166 | 62.9 |
|  | No | 98 | 37.1 |

|  | Minimum | Maximum | Mean | SD |
|--|---------|---------|------|-----|
| Age | 64 | 82 | 71.6 | 4.2 |
| Years of Education | 5 | 23 | 10.4 | 3.2 |
| Income (thousands) | 2 | 61 | 13.2 | 7.3 |
| Hours of Church Participation Per Week | 0 | 20 | 3.6 | 4.2 |

the time of their interview. Twenty-three percent were living alone; 18 percent were living with family; and 9 percent were living alone. Sixty-three percent of the sample were church members.

The respondents ranged in age from 64 to 82 years, with a mean of 71.6 years (SD = 4.2). Years of education completed ranged from 5 to 23, with a mean of 10.4 years. Thus the typical respondent was not a high school graduate. Yearly income ranged from $2,000 to $61,000, with a mean of $13,200 (SD = $7,300). Hours of church participation per week ranged from 0 to 20, with a mean of 3.6 hours (SD = 4.2).

Table 6.2 presents frequency distribution or descriptive statistics on respondents' self-perceptions of health, income adequacy, religiosity, life satisfaction, and family role involvement.

Over 80 percent of the sample rated their health as good or

Table 6.2. Respondent Self-Ratings of Health, Adequacy of Income, Degree of Religiosity, Life Satisfaction, and Family Role Involvement

| Variable | Value | N | % |
|---|---|---|---|
| Self-Rated Health | Poor | 2 | 0.8 |
| | Fair | 50 | 18.9 |
| | Good | 131 | 49.6 |
| | Excellent | 87 | 30.7 |
| Self-Rated Adequacy of Income | Not Adequate | 25 | 30.7 |
| | More or Less | 110 | 41.7 |
| | Adequate | 129 | 48.9 |
| Self-Rated Degree of Religiosity | Strong Disagree | 35 | 13.3 |
| | Disagree | 67 | 25.4 |
| | Neither | 88 | 33.3 |
| | Agree | 62 | 23.5 |
| | Strong Agree | 12 | 4.5 |

| | Minimum | Maximum | Mean | SD |
|---|---|---|---|---|
| Life Satisfaction | 5 | 25 | 15.4 | 5.4 |
| Family Role Involvement Score | 0 | 14 | 6.8 | 3.5 |

excellent. Nearly half felt their income was adequate, and another 42 percent indicated that their income was "more or less adequate." The modal response to the statement, "I am a religious person" was "neither agree nor disagree" (33 percent). Scores on the Diener Life Satisfaction Scale corresponded to the theoretical range of the scale, 5 to 25. The mean life satisfaction score, 15.4, corresponds to a per item mean of just over 3, which places the response directly in the middle of the five-point Likert-type response scale. The average family role involvement scale score was 6.8 (SD), which means that the typical respondent reported an average of nearly seven activities engaged in or services performed for family members on a regular basis each week.

## Comparison of Male and Female Respondents

Table 6.3 presents frequency distributions on categorical scale background variables for male and female respondents. The table also presents the results of chi-square tests carried out to determine the significance of gender differences on these variables.

The data in Table 6.3 indicate that male and female respondents differed significantly on employment status ($\chi^2 = 12.89$, df = 3, p < .01), occupational level ($\chi^2 = 7.06$, df = 2, p < .05), current living situation ($\chi^2 = 10.66$, df = 3, p < .05), and church membership ($\chi^2 = 12.01$, df = 1, p < .001).

The majority of respondents of each sex (58.3 percent) described themselves as retired. Females were more likely to describe themselves as unemployed (26.7 percent) than males (12.5 percent). Males were more likely to be employed full-time or part-time (29.2 percent) than females (15.0 percent). The great majority of respondents of both genders were blue collar workers, but the male sample contained a few professionals (5.6 percent), whereas the female sample did not. Males were more likely to be living with a spouse (58.3 percent) than females (40.0 percent). Females were more likely to be church members (74.2 percent) than males (53.0 percent).

Table 6.3. Employment Status, Occupational Level, Living Situation, and Church Membership by Sex

| Variable | Value | Males | | Females | | $\chi^2$ | p |
|---|---|---|---|---|---|---|---|
| | | N | % | N | % | | |
| Employment | Full-Time | 23 | 16.0 | 11 | 9.2 | 12.89 | .005 |
| Status | Part-Time | 19 | 13.2 | 7 | 5.8 | | |
| | Unemployed | 18 | 12.5 | 32 | 26.7 | | |
| | Retired | 84 | 58.3 | 70 | 58.3 | | |
| Occupational | Professional | 8 | 5.6 | 0 | 0.0 | | |
| Level | White Collar | 20 | 13.9 | 20 | 16.7 | 7.06 | .029 |
| | Blue Collar | 116 | 80.6 | 100 | 83.3 | | |
| Living | Alone | 28 | 19.4 | 32 | 26.7 | | |
| Situation | With Spouse | 84 | 58.3 | 48 | 40.0 | 10.66 | .014 |
| | With Family | 24 | 16.7 | 24 | 20.0 | | |
| | Non-Family | 8 | 5.6 | 16 | 13.3 | | |
| Church | Yes | 77 | 53.5 | 89 | 74.2 | | |
| Member | No | 67 | 46.5 | 31 | 25.8 | 12.01 | .001 |

Table 6.4 presents the results of independent sample t-tests comparing male and female respondents on interval scale background variables. These tests indicated that female respondents were significantly higher than males on years of education ($t = -2.09$, df = 262, $p < .05$), hours per week of church attendance ($t = -7.27$, df = 262, $p < .001$), and family role involvement ($t = -3.35$, df = 262, $p = .001$).

Table 6.5 presents the results of chi-square tests comparing male and female respondents on self-rated health, self-rated income adequacy, and self-rated religiosity. The two sexes differed significantly on two of these three variables, self-rated health ($\chi^2 = 11.12$, df = 3, $p < .05$) and self-rated religiosity ($\chi^2 = 28.70$, df = 4, $p < .001$). Women were more likely to rate their health as excellent, and more likely to agree or strongly agree that they are religious individuals.

Thus female and male respondents differed markedly on most demographic measures, and they also differed on some important

Table 6.4. Age, Education, Income, Weekly Hours of Church Attendance, Life Satisfaction, and Family Role Involvement by Sex

| Variable | Males (N=144) | | Females (N=120) | | t | p |
|---|---|---|---|---|---|---|
| | Mean | SD | Mean | SD | | |
| Age in Years | 71.3 | 4.3 | 72.0 | 4.0 | -1.49 | .137 |
| Years of Education | 10.0 | 3.4 | 10.8 | 2.9 | -12.09 | .038 |
| Annual Income (thousands) | 12.8 | 8.8 | 13.6 | 5.0 | -0.99 | .325 |
| Hours of Church Attendance per Week | 2.1 | 2.9 | 5.6 | 4.8 | -7.27 | .000 |
| Life Satisfaction | 15.6 | 5.5 | 15.0 | 5.3 | 0.86 | .391 |
| Family Role Involvement | 6.2 | 3.2 | 7.6 | 3.6 | -3.35 | .001 |

Table 6.5. Self-Rated Health, Income Adequacy, and Religiosity by Sex

| Variable | Value | Males | | Females | | $\chi^2$ | p |
|---|---|---|---|---|---|---|---|
| | | N | % | N | % | | |
| Self-Rated Health | Poor | 0 | 0.0 | 2 | 1.7 | | |
| | Fair | 36 | 25.0 | 14 | 11.7 | 11.12 | .011 |
| | Good | 71 | 49.3 | 60 | 50.0 | | |
| | Excellent | 37 | 25.7 | 44 | 36.7 | | |
| Self-Rated Income Adequacy | Not Adequate | 16 | 11.1 | 9 | 7.5 | | |
| | More or Less | 67 | 46.5 | 43 | 35.8 | 5.44 | .066 |
| | Adequate | 61 | 42.4 | 68 | 56.7 | | |
| Self-Rated Religiosity | Strongly Disagree | 29 | 20.1 | 6 | 5.0 | | |
| | Disagree | 39 | 27.1 | 28 | 23.3 | | |
| | Neither | 51 | 35.4 | 37 | 30.8 | 28.70 | .000 |
| | Agree | 24 | 16.7 | 38 | 31.7 | | |
| | Strongly Agree | 1 | 0.7 | 11 | 9.2 | | |

self-perception variables. For this reason, the relationships between life satisfaction and the predictors were evaluated separately for male and female respondents.

## Correlations of Life Satisfaction with the Predictors

Table 6.6 presents the zero-order correlations between life satisfaction and the predictor variables for male and female respondents. Among males, two of the nine correlations were significant. Life satisfaction was correlated positively with annual income ($r = .22$, $p < .05$) and weekly hours of church involvement ($r = .28$, $p < .001$). Among females, life satisfaction was correlated positively with weekly hours of church involvement ($r = .56$, $p < .001$), family role involvement ($r = .20$, $p < .05$), and self-rated religiosity ($r = .41$, $p < .001$).

Table 6.6. Correlations Between Life Satisfaction and Predictors, by Sex

|  | Males (N=144) | Females (N=120) |
|---|---|---|
| *Age* | .00 | −.17 |
| *Years of Education* | .11 | −.13 |
| *Annual Income* | .22** | .07 |
| *Weekly Hours of Church Involvement* | .28*** | .56*** |
| *Family Role Involvement* | .01 | .20* |
| *Self-Rated Health* | .03 | .04 |
| *Self-Rated Adequacy of Income* | .05 | .07 |
| *Self-Rated Degree of Religiosity* | .16 | .41*** |
| *Occupational Level* | −.18 | −.07 |

*p < .05
**p < .01
***p < .001

## Regression of Life Satisfaction: Males

Table 6.7 presents the results of the stepwise multiple regression of life satisfaction on the nine predictors for male respondents. The data in the table indicate that two of the nine predictors made significant (p < .05) contributions to the prediction of life satisfaction: hours of church attendance (t = 3.53, p < .001) and annual income (t = 2.53, p < .05).

## Regression of Life Satisfaction: Females

Table 6.8 presents the regression of life satisfaction on nine predictors among female respondents. The data in the table indicate that two of the nine predictors made significant (p < .05) contributions to the prediction of life satisfaction among elderly black women: hours of church attendance (t = 5.50, p < .001) and self-rated religiosity (t = 2.21, p < .05). Together these predictors accounted for 34 percent of the variability in the life satisfaction of elderly black women.

Table 6.7. Regression of Life Satisfaction on Nine Predictors: Male Respondents

*Analysis of Variance of Regression*

| Source | SS | df | MS | F |
|---|---|---|---|---|
| Regression | 513.1 | 2 | 256.5 | 9.87*** |
| Residual | 3640.6 | 140 | 26.0 | |

*Summary Table*

| Step | Variable | R | R² | Beta | t |
|---|---|---|---|---|---|
| 1. | Hours of Church | .29 | .08 | .28 | 3.53*** |
| 2. | Annual Income | .35 | .12 | .20 | 2.53* |

*p<.05
***p<.001

Table 6.8. Regression of Life Satisfaction on Nine Predictors: Female Respondents

*Analysis of Variance of Regression*

| Source | SS | df | MS | F |
|---|---|---|---|---|
| Regression | 1150.2 | 2 | 575.1 | 30.00*** |
| Residual | 2242.6 | 117 | 19.2 | |

*Summary Table*

| Step | Variable | R | R2 | Beta | t |
|---|---|---|---|---|---|
| 1. | Hours of Church | .56 | .31 | .47 | 5.50*** |
| 2. | Self-Rated Religiosity | .58 | .34 | .19 | 2.21* |

*p<.01
***p<.001

## SUMMARY

Elderly black women are more likely than elderly black men to attend church and are more heavily involved in family roles. They also rated themselves as healthier than men and more religious than men.

Among males, weekly hours of church involvement and annual income were significant zero-order predictors of life satisfaction. Among females, significant zero-order predictors of life satisfaction were weekly hours of church involvement, family role involvement, and self-rated degree of religiosity.

Among males, the combination of church involvement and annual income explained 12 percent of the variability in life satisfaction. Among females, the combination of church involvement and self-rated religiosity explained 34 percent of the variability in life satisfaction.

Chapter 7

# An Empirical Investigation of the Predictors of Life Satisfaction Among the Black Elderly: Additional Findings

In order to identify the correlates of life satisfaction within specific segments of the elderly black population, a series of correlational analyses were conducted. Correlations between life satisfaction and the several predictor variables in the model were calculated for subsamples of the participating black elderly. These subsamples were defined by the participants' current employment status, occupational level, current living situation, church membership status, age cohort, and level of education. Through these analyses it was hoped that it might be possible to identify predictors of life satisfaction that had special relevance for specific groups of the black elderly. Such data could be of use to both social workers and social policy planners in their efforts to meet the needs of this population.

## EMPLOYMENT STATUS

It was anticipated that there might be differences in the factors predicting life satisfaction among respondents who reported themselves to be still working (full- or part-time), unemployed, and retired. Table 7.1 presents the correlations between life satis-

Table 7.1. Correlations Between Life Satisfaction and Predictors, by Sex: Respondents Currently Employed Full-Time or Part-Time

| Predictor | Males (N = 42) | Females (N = 18) |
|---|---|---|
| Age | .01 | -.12 |
| Years of Education | .10 | -.67** |
| Annual Income | .34* | .67** |
| Weekly Hours of Church Involvement | .37* | .72*** |
| Family Role Involvement | .01 | -.04 |
| Self-Rated Health | -.03 | .47* |
| Self-Rated Adequacy of Income | .03 | ___(a) |
| Self-Rated Degree of Religiosity | .37* | .50* |
| Occupational Level(b) | -.53*** | .02 |

* p < .05
** p < .01
*** p < .001
(a) no correlation calculated due to zero variability on income adequacy rating
(b) over lifespan

faction and the predictor variables for those participants who were still working full- or part-time at the time of the survey.

Among the employed males, life satisfaction was related positively to annual income (r = .34, p < .05), weekly hours of church involvement (r = .37, p < .05), and self-rated degree of religiosity (r = .37, p < .05). Life satisfaction was related negatively to occupational level within this group (r = -.53, p < .001). The positive relationships found within this group are generally consistent with the findings obtained for the entire male sample, but the negative relationship between occupational level and life satisfaction is somewhat surprising. The finding suggests that among men who are still working, satisfaction tends to be lower among those who had white collar jobs than among those who held blue collar jobs throughout their lives. (There were no males in the study sample who indicated that they had held professional level employment over the course of their lives.) It is possible that men who had white collar jobs but who are still working at this point in their lives had been relatively unsuccessful at their jobs, and were thus unable to retire, as the great majority of their peers did. This could lead to a self-perception as a failure and a concomitant lack of satisfaction with life. In contrast, the blue collar workers might not feel that they should have been able to retire comfortably, since they had probably struggled financially throughout the course of their lives.

Among the few women in the sample who were still working part- or full-time, life satisfaction was also related positively to annual income ($r = .67$, $p < .01$), to weekly hours of church involvement ($r = .72$, $p < .01$), and to self-rated religiosity ($r = .50$, $p < .05$). In addition, life satisfaction was related positively to self-rated health ($r = .47$, $p < .05$) and negatively to years of education ($r = -.67$, $p < .01$). There was no significant relationship between occupational level and life satisfaction among the employed women. It is possible that the women in the sample did not feel any sense of inadequacy relative to their peers if they found themselves unable to retire. It is also possible that some of these women had relatively high level jobs which they valued for the intrinsic rewards of the work, rather than simply for the extrinsic benefits such as salary and benefits. However, the negative relationship between years of education and life satisfaction among this group suggests that those who had more schooling were not very satisfied. It is possible that education raises one's level of aspiration to the extent that actual accomplishments are held up to a higher standard. It is also possible that those with more education are simply more aware of the discrepancy between what one has achieved and what it is possible to achieve in this society.

Table 7.2 presents the corresponding correlations for those respondents who described themselves as currently unemployed.

Table 7.2. Correlations Between Life Satisfaction and Predictors, by Sex:
Respondents Reporting They Are Currently Unemployed

| Predictor | Males (N=18) | Females (N=32) |
|---|---|---|
| Age | -.11 | .05 |
| Years of Education | .02 | .08 |
| Annual Income | .07 | .42* |
| Weekly Hours of Church Involvement | .42 | .63*** |
| Family Role Involvement | .36 | .34 |
| Self-Rated Health | .27 | .04 |
| Self-Rated Adequacy of Income | -.22 | .04 |
| Self-Rated Degree of Religiosity | -.39 | .52** |
| Occupational Level(a) | -.02 | .02 |

   * p < .05
  ** p < .01
 *** p < .001
(a) over lifespan

This was a relatively small group, so some correlations in the table which are moderate in magnitude are nevertheless nonsignificant, due to the relatively low power associated with correlations based on small samples. Among the unemployed males, none of the observed correlations were statistically significant. Among the unemployed females, significant positive correlations were observed between life satisfaction and annual income ($r = .42$, $p < .05$), weekly hours of church involvement ($r = .63$, $p < .001$), and self-rated degree of religiosity ($r = .52$, $p < .01$).

The largest groups of men and women in the sample identified themselves as retired. Table 7.3 presents the correlations between life satisfaction and the predictors for those in this group. Among the men who were retired, the only significant predictor of life satisfaction was annual income ($r = .40$, $p < .001$). This moderate correlation suggests the importance of financial security for the males. In contrast, among the retired women, there was actually

Table 7.3. Correlations Between Life Satisfaction and Predictors, by Sex: Respondents Reporting that They Are Retired

| Predictor | Males (N=83) | Females (N=70) |
|---|---|---|
| Age | .02 | -.31** |
| Years of Education | .20 | -.19 |
| Annual Income | .40*** | -.29* |
| Weekly Hours of Church Involvement | .21 | .47*** |
| Family Role Involvement | .00 | .22 |
| Self-Rated Health | .02 | -.06 |
| Self-Rated Adequacy of Income | .03 | .11 |
| Self-Rated Degree of Religiosity | .07 | .33** |
| Occupational Level(a) | -.16 | -.14 |

*p < .05
**p < .01
***p < .001
(a) over lifespan

a negative relationship between life satisfaction and annual income. This could be interpreted as indicating a tendency on the part of the women to have a somewhat other-worldly orientation. This conclusion is supported by the significant positive correlation observed for this group between life satisfaction and self-rated degree of religiosity (r = .33, p < .05). However, it is also possible that women with lower annual incomes might be called upon more often by their families to fill important roles, and it is also possible that those with lower incomes rely more heavily on the church for certain services, which in turn would open up other avenues for satisfying activities. Life satisfaction among retired women was related positively, but not significantly, to family role involvement (r = .22, p > .05), but a significant positive relationship was observed between life satisfaction and weekly hours of church involvement (r = .47, p < .001).

Among the retired women a negative relationship was

observed between age and life satisfaction (r = -.31, p < .01). This indicates that retired women may become less satisfied with life as they grow older. This could be associated with a process of disappointment regarding the expected rewards of retirement. The younger women who have retired more recently may be enjoying the leisure and relaxation, but after a few years of relative inactivity retirement may lose some of its appeal.

The findings described in this section indicate that special attention may be warranted for older black males who are continuing to work because they are not in a position to retire. It may be that these individuals could benefit from interventions aimed at helping them to understand the economic exigencies of our society and assisting them to view their continued employment in a more positive light. The findings obtained for retired women suggest that life after retirement may not be as fulfilling as some individuals anticipate. This suggests a possible need for pre-retirement counseling, and perhaps a policy of delaying retirement where possible for those who are physically able to continue to work.

## OCCUPATIONAL LEVEL

Respondents reported whether they had held professional, white collar, or blue collar jobs during the greatest portion of their professional lives. Relatively few respondents described themselves as having held jobs in the two higher categories. Table 7.4 presents the correlations between life satisfaction and the predictors for professionals and white collar employees. The males represented in the table are actually all white collar employees, since there were no professional males in the sample. There were female professionals (N = 8).

The data in Table 7.4 indicate that among white collar males self-rated adequacy of income was a strong predictor of life satisfaction (r = .66, p < .001). This again suggests that finances

Table 7.4. Correlations Between Life Satisfaction and Predictors, by Sex: Respondents Reporting that They Held Professional or White Collar Jobs Over Their Lifespans

| Predictor | Males (N=28) | Females (N=20) |
|---|---|---|
| Age | .35 | -.76*** |
| Years of Education | -.27 | .76*** |
| Annual Income | -.22 | .79*** |
| Weekly Hours of Church Involvement | -.05 | .14 |
| Family Role Involvement | -.03 | -.07 |
| Self-Rated Health | -.47* | -.04 |
| Self-Rated Adequacy of Income | .66*** | -.53* |
| Self-Rated Degree of Religiosity | .18 | .27 |

$^*$ p < .05
$^{**}$ p < .01
$^{***}$ p < .001

are quite important for the men. Inexplicably, self-rated health was related negatively to life satisfaction (r = -.47, p < .05). Perhaps these white collar employees are literally willing to give up their health in order to achieve financial security. Among the professional and white collar women in the sample life satisfaction was related strongly to both years of education (r = .76, p < .001) and annual income (r = .79, p < .001). However, life satisfaction was related negatively to self-rated adequacy of income (r = -.53, p < .05). This suggests that the professional and white collar women in the sample derive satisfaction from their work itself, rather than simply the salary. Women who have more education would naturally tend to have higher level jobs that pay more, but the perception that one's income is adequate is actually associated with lower levels of satisfaction.

Table 7.5 presents the correlations between life satisfaction and the predictors for the much larger samples of men and women who reported having held blue collar jobs over the

Table 7.5. Correlations Between Life Satisfaction and Predictors, by Sex: Respondents Reporting that They Held Blue Collar Jobs Over Their Lifespans

| Predictor | Males (N=116) | Females (N=100) |
|---|---|---|
| Age | -.08 | -.06 |
| Years of Education | .01 | -.25* |
| Annual Income | .37*** | -.06 |
| Weekly Hours of Church Involvement | .32*** | .62*** |
| Family Role Involvement | .03 | .25* |
| Self-Rated Health | .10 | .05 |
| Self-Rated Adequacy of Income | -.06 | .17 |
| Self-Rated Degree of Religiosity | .22* | .43*** |

* p < .05
** p < .01
*** p < .001

course of their lifetimes. The correlations observed for these respondents were very different from those observed for the professional and white collar workers. Among blue collar males, life satisfaction was related to the now familiar triad of annual income (r = .37, p < .001), weekly hours of church involvement (r = .32,  p < .001), and self-rated degree of religiosity (r = .22, p < .05). Among the blue collar females, significant positive correlations were also observed between life satisfaction and both weekly hours of church involvement (r = .62, p < .001) and self-rated degree of religiosity (r = .43, p < .001). However, the other significant correlation observed for the blue collar females was a significant negative correlation between years of education and life satisfaction (r = -.25, p < .05). This correlation makes good sense, since an individual having substantial education but a blue collar job might be expected to be somewhat disappointed with what she had accomplished in her life.

These findings indicate substantial differences in the factors that predict life satisfaction among elderly blacks having different occupational levels. Those with professional or white collar employment histories appear to be much more concerned with income, whether it is actual income (as in the case of the women) or self-perceived adequacy of income (as in the case of the men). In contrast, those with blue collar work histories appear to be much more concerned with church participation and religion as factors determining life satisfaction.

## *CURRENT LIVING SITUATION*

Three groups of respondents were examined with respect to current living status: those living alone; those living with a spouse; and those living with family or non-family members in common household. It was anticipated that the correlations between life satisfaction and the predictors might be quite different for the individuals in these three groups.

Table 7.6 presents the correlations for those respondents who reported living alone. Among the males in this group, life satisfaction was related positively to self-rated adequacy of income ($r = .42$, $p < .05$) and to occupational level ($r = .49$, $p < .01$). No significant correlations were observed for these males between life satisfaction and either church or family involvement. In contrast, among the women who reported living alone, life satisfaction was related strongly to church involvement ($r = .69$, $p < .001$) and moderately to both family role involvement ($r = .45$, $p < .01$) and self- rated degree of religiosity ($r = .40$, $p < .05$).

Table 7.7 presents the correlations between life satisfaction and the predictors for those respondents who reported living with a spouse. Among the males in this group, the correlations were quite different from those observed among males living alone. Life satisfaction was related positively to annual income ($r = .35$, $p < .001$) and weekly hours of church involvement ($r = .41$, $p < .001$), but negatively to occupational level ($r = -.24$, $p < .05$).

Table 7.6. Correlations Between Life Satisfaction and Predictors, by Sex: Respondents Reporting that They Live Alone

| Predictor | Males (N=28) | Females (N=32) |
|---|---|---|
| Age | -.14 | .01 |
| Years of Education | -.29 | -.32 |
| Annual Income | -.24 | .22 |
| Weekly Hours of Church Involvement | .00 | .69*** |
| Family Role Involvement | .21 | .45** |
| Self-Rated Health | -.07 | .08 |
| Self-Rated Adequacy of Income | .42* | .06 |
| Self-Rated Degree of Religiosity | .21 | .40* |
| Occupational Level(a) | .49** | .02 |

   * p < .05
  ** p < .01
 *** p < .001
(a) over lifespan


Table 7.7. Correlations Between Life Satisfaction and Predictors, by Sex: Respondents Reporting that They Live with a Spouse

| Predictor | Males (N=84) | Females (N=48) |
|---|---|---|
| Age | -.19 | -.58*** |
| Years of Education | -.09 | -.18 |
| Annual Income | .35*** | -.06 |
| Weekly Hours of Church Involvement | .41*** | .56*** |
| Family Role Involvement | -.07 | .20 |
| Self-Rated Health | .16 | .17 |
| Self-Rated Adequacy of Income | .08 | .06 |
| Self-Rated Degree of Religiosity | .18 | .58*** |
| Occupational Level(a) | -.24* | -.10 |

   * p < .05
  ** p < .01
 *** p < .001
(a) over lifespan

Among the females living with a spouse, life satisfaction was related positively to church involvement (r = .56, p < .001) and to self-rated degree of religiosity (r = .58, p < .001), but negatively to age (r = -.58, p < .001). Thus church and religion were as important for women living with a spouse as they were for women living alone, but family role involvement was more important for the women who were living alone.

A still different picture emerges for those respondents who were living with someone other than a spouse (either family or non-family). Table 7.8 presents the correlations of the predictors with life satisfaction for this group. Among males, life satisfaction was related positively to age (r = .56, p < .001) and negatively to occupational level (r = -.40, p < .05). Among the women in this group, the only significant predictor of life satisfaction was weekly hours of church involvement (r = .45, p < .01).

These findings imply that the needs of black elderly in differ-

Table 7.8. Correlations Between Life Satisfaction and Predictors, by Sex: Respondents Reporting that They Live with Someone Other Than a Spouse

| Predictor | Males (N=32) | Females (N=40) |
|---|---|---|
| Age | .56*** | .07 |
| Years of Education | .34 | -.16 |
| Annual Income | .42 | .01 |
| Weekly Hours of Church Involvement | .10 | .45** |
| Family Role Involvement | .14 | -.23 |
| Self-Rated Health | -.41* | -.30 |
| Self-Rated Adequacy of Income | .14 | .30 |
| Self-Rated Degree of Religiosity | .06 | .14 |
| Occupational Level(a) | -.40* | -.20 |

\* p < .05
\*\* p < .01
\*\*\* p < .001
(a) over lifespan

ent living situations vary substantially, and that interventions aimed at promoting the well-being of this population need to take into consideration the individual's type of household. The one element that is consistent across these living situation groups is the importance of church participation for women.

## CHURCH MEMBERSHIP

Correlations between life satisfaction and the predictor variables were also calculated separately for respondents who were and were not church members. Table 7.9 presents the correlations for church members, and Table 7.10 presents the correlations for those who are not church members. The two sets of correlations are quite different. Within the church member group, male respondents demonstrated significant positive correlations between life satisfaction

Table 7.9. Correlations Between Life Satisfaction and Predictors, by Sex: Respondents Reporting that They Are Church Members

| Predictor | Males (N=77) | Females (N=89) |
|---|---|---|
| Age | .06 | -.16 |
| Years of Education | .17 | -.03 |
| Annual Income | .32** | .07 |
| Weekly Hours of Church Involvement | .32** | .35*** |
| Family Role Involvement | .03 | .06 |
| Self-Rated Health | .13 | .08 |
| Self-Rated Adequacy of Income | .08 | -.05 |
| Self-Rated Degree of Religiosity | -.05 | .15 |
| Occupational Level(a) | -.17 | .01 |

* p < .05
** p < .01
*** p < .001
(a) over lifespan

Table 7.10. Correlations Between Life Satisfaction and Predictors, by Sex: Respondents Reporting that They Are Not Church Members

| Predictor | Males (N=67) | Females (N=31) |
|---|---|---|
| Age | -.08 | .26 |
| Years of Education | .05 | -.13 |
| Annual Income | .18 | -.19 |
| Family Role Involvement | .03 | .06 |
| Self-Rated Health | -.09 | -.10 |
| Self-Rated Adequacy of Income | -.01 | .03 |
| Self-Rated Degree of Religiosity | .24* | -.17 |
| Occupational Level(a) | -.17 | .02 |

* p < .05
(a) over lifespan

and both annual income (r = .32, p < .01) and weekly hours of church involvement (r = .32, p < .01). Female church members manifested only a single significant predictor of life satisfaction, weekly hours of church involvement (r = .35, p < .01). Among the non-church members, weekly hours of church involvement was not relevant and so could not be related to life satisfaction. Paradoxically, the only significant relationship observed in Table 7.10 was a significant positive relationship among the males between self-rated degree of religiosity and life satisfaction (r = .24, p < .05). This was a weak correlation and is perhaps nothing more than a Type I error. However, it is possible that the relationship indicates a perception on the part of some males that one can be religious without being a member of a church.

## THE YOUNG OLD AND THE OLD OLD

Based on the frequency distribution of age within the total sample, the respondents were classified as falling into either a younger group, aged 64 through 70, or an older group, aged 71 and above. Correlations between life satisfaction and the predictors were obtained for each of these groups separately. Table 7.11 presents the correlations for the 64- to 70-year-old group. Among the men in this group, life satisfaction was related to both annual income (r = .44, p < .001) and weekly hours of church involvement (r = .37, p < .001). Among the women more significant relationships were observed. Life satisfaction was related most strongly to weekly hours of church involvement (r = .60, p < .001) and self-rated degree of religiosity (r = .55, p < .01). In addition, life satisfaction among the women was related negatively to age (r = -.48, p < .01), years of education (r = -.30, p < .05), and occupational level.

Table 7.12 presents the corresponding correlations for those 71 and older. The correlations are quite different for the younger group. Among the older males, neither annual income nor weekly hours of church involvement is related significantly to

Table 7.11. Correlations Between Life Satisfaction and Predictors, by Sex: Respondents Aged 64 through 70

| Predictor | Males (N=79) | Females (N=51) |
|---|---|---|
| Age | .00 | -.48** |
| Years of Education | -.07 | -.30* |
| Annual Income | .44*** | .08 |
| Weekly Hours of Church Involvement | .37*** | .60*** |
| Family Role Involvement | -.12 | -.10 |
| Self-Rated Health | -.09 | -.10 |
| Self-Rated Adequacy of Income | .18 | .17 |
| Self-Rated Degree of Religiosity | .13 | .55** |
| Occupational Level(a) | -.16 | -.36** |

* p < .05
** p < .01
*** p < .001
(a) over lifespan

Table 7.12. Correlations Between Life Satisfaction and Predictors, by Sex: Respondents Aged 71 or Over

| Predictor | Males (N=65) | Females (N=69) |
|---|---|---|
| Age | -.34** | .24* |
| Years of Education | .19 | .04 |
| Annual Income | .13 | .05 |
| Weekly Hours of Church Involvement | .21 | .56*** |
| Family Role Involvement | .45*** | .34** |
| Self-Rated Health | -.02 | .11 |
| Self-Rated Adequacy of Income | -.09 | -.01 |
| Self-Rated Degree of Religiosity | .24 | .27* |
| Occupational Level(a) | -.17 | .13 |

* p < .05
** p < .01
*** p < .001
(a) over lifespan

life satisfaction. Instead, family role involvement is related positively to life satisfaction (r = .45, p < .001). In addition, age is related negatively to life satisfaction, indicating that life satisfaction tends to decrease as the old grow older. Among the females in the older group, both weekly hours of church involvement (r = .56, p < .001) and family role involvement (r = .34, p < .01) are related positively to life satisfaction. Self-rated degree of religiosity is also related positively to life satisfaction (r = .27, p < .05). Finally, among females in the older group, age was related positively to life satisfaction (r = .24, p < .05).

Thus it would appear that as men grow older they become somewhat less concerned with their income. Moreover, as men and women grow older, they become more concerned with their involvement in their families.

## EDUCATIONAL LEVEL

The final background variable on which the sample was divided for analysis was educational level. Based on the frequency distribution of years of education completed, the samples of male and female respondents were divided into those who had not completed high school and those who had. Once again, the predictors of life satisfaction in these two groups turned out to be somewhat different. Table 7.13 presents the correlations for those respondents who were not high school graduates. The data in the table indicate that among the males in this sample life satisfaction was related significantly to annual income ($r = .50$, $p < .001$) and weekly hours of church involvement ($r = .31$, $p < .001$). Among the women in this sample life satisfaction was related positively weekly hours of church involvement ($r = .39$, $p < .01$) and to self-rated health ($r = .35$, $p < .05$). Life satisfaction among the less-educated

Table 7.13. Correlations Between Life Satisfaction and Predictors, by Sex: Respondents Reporting that They Are Not High School Graduates

| Predictor | Males (N=104) | Females (N=46) |
|---|---|---|
| Age | -.10 | -.47*** |
| Years of Education | -.09 | -.39** |
| Annual Income | .50*** | -.01 |
| Weekly Hours of Church Involvement | .31*** | .39** |
| Family Role Involvement | .01 | .07 |
| Self-Rated Health | .17 | .35* |
| Self-Rated Adequacy of Income | .01 | .15 |
| Self-Rated Degree of Religiosity | .14 | .15 |
| Occupational Level(a) | -.08 | .11 |

  * p < .05
 ** p < .01
*** p < .001
(a) over lifespan

women was related negatively to their age (r = -.47, p < .001) and their years of education (r = -.39, p < .01). Thus even within the group who were not high school graduates there was variability in life satisfaction associated with the years of education they had.

Table 7.14 presents the correlations between life satisfaction and the predictors for the respondents who were high school graduates. Among the males in this group, life satisfaction was not related significantly to annual income, or weekly hours of church involvement, or family role involvement. Life satisfaction was related positively to self-rated degree of religiosity (r = .42, p < .01), and it was related negatively to self-rated health (r = -.46, p < .01). In contrast, among the females in the better educated group, life satisfaction was related positively to weekly hours of church involvement (r = .64, p < .001), self-rated degree of religiosity (r = .56, p < .001), and family role involvement (r = .30, p < .01). Life

Table 7.14. Correlations Between Life Satisfaction and Predictors, by Sex: Respondents Reporting that They Are High School Graduates

| Predictor | Males (N=40) | Females (N=74) |
|---|---|---|
| Age | .24 | -.06 |
| Years of Education | -.16 | -.30** |
| Annual Income | -.20 | .09 |
| Weekly Hours of Church Involvement | .20 | .64*** |
| Family Role Involvement | .19 | .30** |
| Self-Rated Health | -.46** | -.12 |
| Self-Rated Adequacy of Income | .02 | .03 |
| Self-Rated Degree of Religiosity | .42** | .56*** |
| Occupational Level(a) | -.05 | -.38*** |

\* p < .05
\*\* p < .01
\*\*\* p < .001
(a) over lifespan

satisfaction among the better educated women was related negatively to years of education (r = -.30, p < .01) and to occupational level (r = -.38, p < .001).

## SUMMARY

The data presented in this chapter indicate two important conclusions, one of which involves a generalization, and the other of which cautions against overgeneralization. It does appear that a relatively consistent distinction between male and female respondents runs throughout the data: Males appear to be much more like to be concerned with financial issues, including both actual annual income and perceived adequacy of income. In contrast, the women in the sample seem to have an almost other-worldly disdain for money, occasionally even demonstrating negative relationships between income measures and life satisfaction. On the other hand, the more important conclusion to be drawn from the material in this chapter is that one must be cautious in generalizing regarding the predictors of life satisfaction among elderly blacks. We are not discussing a homogeneous population here. Just as there are differences in the predictors based on gender, so there are substantial differences based on employment status, occupational level, current living situation, church membership, age, and educational attainment. The factors that predict life satisfaction for one elderly black individual may be quite different from those which predict satisfaction for another. In the final analysis, it is the responsibility of the practitioner to be sufficiently familiar with the circumstances of the individual so as to make informed interventions.

# Chapter 8

# A Policy Framework
# for Elderly Black Americans

In this chapter the results of the empirical investigation of the correlates of life satisfaction will be summarized and used to generate policy recommendations for agencies charged with providing services to the black elderly.

## *OVERVIEW OF FINDINGS*

The empirical investigation reported in the previous chapter indicated many differences between male and female respondents. The elderly black males in the sample were significantly more likely than their female counterparts to still be employed full- or part-time, and the men were more likely to report having professional or white collar jobs over the course of their careers. The males were also more likely to be living with a spouse, as opposed to living alone or with one's family. The female respondents were more likely to be church members (74.2 percent) than the males (53.5 percent).

As a group, the female respondents had slightly more education (mean = 10.8 years) than the males (mean = 10.0 years). The women reported a higher mean number of hours of church attendance than the males, and the women had significantly higher scores for family role involvement. In addition, female respondents perceived themselves as healthier and more religious than the males.

Interestingly, men and women did not differ significantly on satisfaction with life. This suggests that the factors predicting life satisfaction among men were likely to be quite different from those predicting life satisfaction among women.

Correlations and regression analyses carried out separately for male and female respondents confirmed this expectation in part. Among males, satisfaction with life was predicted by actual annual income and by weekly hours of church activity. Among females, satisfaction with life was related to weekly hours of church involvement, self-rated religiosity, and family role involvement. Thus male and female respondents differed in several areas, but they had in common the relationship between church participation and subjective well-being.

## DISCUSSION

These findings support the conclusions of Taylor (1985) and Taylor and Chatters (1986) regarding the importance of the church and religion among many African-American seniors. The findings also support the assertions of Clavon and Smith (1986) and Morrisson (1982) regarding the significance of the family and extended family. Clearly the social history of African-American people in America suggests that church and family represent important sources of strength and support, and the results of this study show that involvement in church and family roles are associated with life satisfaction as well.

An interesting conclusion suggested by the findings of the present study has to do with the nature of the relationship between family and church involvement and life satisfaction. Whereas Taylor (1985) emphasized the services received from the church as providing valuable support to elderly members, the interview responses of the African-American seniors in the present study clearly suggested that providing assistance to fellow church members and helping perform necessary work for the church were important sources of satisfaction. Similarly, re-spondents indicated that they provided many different forms of service and assistance for the members of their family, and that such service was an important factor in making seniors feel important and useful. These data clearly support the theories of Rosow (1973) regarding the importance of the roles that the individual performs in giving meaning to life. A senior citizen who visits a sick church member or offers financial assistance to a grandchild attending college is likely to gain a sense of personal worth by virtue of these efforts. Persons who have the opportunity to perform such services are likely to receive much positive feedback for their efforts, and they are likely also to have a sense of personal effectiveness.

These conclusions are supported by comments made by re-spondents during the course of the interviews. Many of the participants remarked that participating in the good works of the church was a significant source of pride and personal satisfaction. Others suggested that these activities kept them busy and occupied and provided a structure to their lives. Several respondents stated explicitly that the church was a community for them and that they felt both an obligation to contribute to that community and a sense of security that they would be cared for by the community if that became necessary.

It is interesting that self-rated religiosity was a significant predictor of life satisfaction for women, but not for men. It is possible that it is more socially acceptable for women to adopt an other-world perspective, whereas men must maintain a more pragmatic and utilitarian stance. This interpretation is consistent with the finding that life satisfaction among male respondents was related to income, although no such relationship was found for women. This interpretation is also supported by the responses of one male who maintained earnestly that he was not truly a religious individual, but rather participated in church activities because it was "good for business." This man was a painting contractor by trade and he indicated that most of his customers were members of his congregation. Interestingly, other seniors interviewed at the same center described him as a very religious individual who contributed significantly to the good works of the church. It is possible that this individual was somewhat embarrassed to reveal his devout and caring side to the interviewer, preferring to be regarded as a perceptive businessman.

The other noteworthy difference between the male and female respondents in this study was the fact that family role involvement was related significantly to life satisfaction among women, but not among men. This may be the result of the fact that the women had a significantly higher mean on the family role involvement measure and, concomitantly, greater variability. It may also have to do with the nature of the activities and services represented in the role involvement measure. In conducting the interviews, it became quite apparent that the types of roles performed by men and women were quite different. Men tended to report engaging in activities with their children and grandchildren. They went to sporting events, took the grandchildren fishing, and went to movies. In contrast, female respondents were more likely to report that they did various forms of work, such as cooking, cleaning, shopping, and ironing. It is possible that such roles provide a more direct sense of efficacy. That is, the women can see readily the results of their efforts and the benefits that accrue to family members. This interpretation would be consistent with Rosow's (1973) role theory and would be consistent with the relationship observed among women between family role involvement and satisfaction with life.

Another possible interpretation is that men may in fact perform many roles such as cleaning and cooking, but may be reluctant to admit that they do. Alternatively, they may perform such roles, but not regard such activities as significant in comparison to other activities, such as sports or fishing. That is, the men may be sex role stereotypical in the reporting of family roles, as well as in the performance of these roles. This issue should be considered in future research to be conducted on this population.

## POLICY RECOMMENDATIONS

Of course, the clearest implication of these findings is that the black church should be relied upon to serve as a vehicle for providing services for the black elderly. It is clearly to the advantage of society to foster the growth of all naturally occurring mechanisms which serve to facilitate the involvement of seniors in meaningful roles and activities. The black church is obviously one such mechanism. Programs conducted with the cooperation of the church aimed at developing foster grandparent relationships, tutoring and tax assistance, provision of hot meals for other seniors, and similar useful activities would appear to be particularly valuable, benefiting those who provide the services as much as those receiving assistance. Seniors would appear to benefit as well from participation in outreach programs aimed at identifying and making contact with other seniors who may be isolated and living with no apparent mission or purpose.

Such programs are, of course, already in place within the black churches of the United States. However, government and private sector financing could be directed toward increasing the capacity of the churches to carry out such good works.

The potential value of such efforts is perhaps increased by the sociodemographic changes that are occurring in the African-American community today. As more young African-Americans assume positions of responsibility and leadership in government and business, they become more mobile. Traditional extended family relationships may be disrupted by job transfers and promotions. In such instances, some family role responsibilities performed by seniors may be lost. Grandpa cannot make breakfast for his grandchildren when they have moved with their parents to another state. In these instances, it may be especially important to provide Grandpa with an opportunity to serve within the context of church-related activities. This might occur through a foster grandparent program, a church-affiliated scouting or sports program, or an after-school tutoring program.

Efforts should be undertaken to establish links between churches and service providers of all types. The churches are likely to be receptive to any efforts that might be beneficial to members of their congregations, including self-help groups, health screenings, food distributions, and community outreach efforts. Service providers should be aware that the churches are strategically located, that they have the physical facilities to hold meetings, and that they are a source of willing talent.

The results of the study also suggest the need to direct attention toward efforts to strengthen the family. Social and economic forces appear to be threatening the traditional black extended family, and it would be tragic if this historical source of strength within the black community were weakened. Efforts aimed at strengthening the family can also be located in the church, in the form of informational meetings concerned with eldercare and intergenerational family relationships. Liaisons with local community mental health centers and with colleges and universities would help to provide the professional support that would be required for such efforts.

# Questionnaire

1.  Your date of birth: _____  _____  _____
                                    month       day       year

2.  Your sex (check one) _____  _____
                                  male    female

3.  Which one of the following best describes your living situation?
    _____ live alone
    _____ live with spouse only
    _____ live with other family
    _____ (specify) _____

    _____
    _____

4.  Total number of persons living in the household _____

5.  Number of dependents _____

6.  Household income $ _____ per year (net)

7.  Highest grade in school you completed _____

8.  What is your current work status? (check one)
    _____ employed full time
    _____ employed part time
    _____ unemployed
    _____ retired
    _____ never employed

9.  What is (was) your principal occupation for most of your life?
    _____

10. How adequate is your family income? (check one)
   _____ not adequate
   _____ more or less adequate
   _____ adequate

11. Would you say your own health, in general is (check one)
   _____ excellent
   _____ fair
   _____ good
   _____ poor

12. Do you attend church (check one)    _____ Yes _____ No
   If so, how often _____

If yes, list below the church activities in which you participate:
   1. _____ Hours per week this activity
   2. _____
   3. _____
   4. _____
   5. _____
   6. _____
   7. _____
   8. _____
   9. _____
   10. _____
   11. _____
   12. _____
   13. _____
   14. _____
   15. _____
   (Use more space on the other side of page, if necessary)

13. On this five-point scale indicate your view by circling the
   appropriate number. (on a scale running from extremely important = 5, to not important = 1)

   How important would you say religion is in your life?

   ____      ____      ____      ____      ____
    1         2         3         4         5

14. I am a religious individual (check one):

| 1 | 2 | 3 | 4 | 5 |
|---|---|---|---|---|
| Strongly Disagree | Disagree | Neither Agree nor Disagree | Agree | Strongly Agree |

15. What does the family mean to you?

_____

_____

_____

16. Now I would like to ask you about your relationships with your family.

First, I would like you to list the individuals whom you consider to be your family (RECORD ON PAGE 107). Identify the person by first name only.

17. Good. Now let's talk about each of these people _____ (First person names), about how many hours per month do you have personal contact with him/her? _____

How about telephone contact? _____

And things you do with _____

And things you do for _____

What does he/she do for you? _____

On a scale of 1 to 5, I would like you to tell me how close you feel to (name) _____.

On this five-point scale, 1 means not very close at all, and 5 means so close that you feel free to tell (name) _____ your innermost secrets.

| 1 | 2 | 3 | 4 | 5 |
|---|---|---|---|---|
| not very close | somewhat close | somewhat distant | close | very close |

18. Please indicate the extent to which you agree or disagree with each of the following statements.

(a) In most ways my life is close to ideal (check one):

| 1 | 2 | 3 | 4 | 5 |
|---|---|---|---|---|
| Strongly Disagree | Disagree | Neither Agree nor Disagree | Agree | Strongly Agree |

(b) The conditions of my life are excellent (check one):

| 1 | 2 | 3 | 4 | 5 |
|---|---|---|---|---|
| Strongly Disagree | Disagree | Neither Agree nor Disagree | Agree | Strongly Agree |

(c) I am satisfied with my life (check one):

| 1 | 2 | 3 | 4 | 5 |
|---|---|---|---|---|
| Strongly Disagree | Disagree | Neither Agree nor Disagree | Agree | Strongly Agree |

(d) So far I have gotten the important things I want in life (check one):

| 1 | 2 | 3 | 4 | 5 |
|---|---|---|---|---|
| Strongly Disagree | Disagree | Neither Agree nor Disagree | Agree | Strongly Agree |

(e) If I could live my life over, I would change almost nothing (check one):

| 1 | 2 | 3 | 4 | 5 |
|---|---|---|---|---|
| Strongly Disagree | Disagree | Neither Agree nor Disagree | Agree | Strongly Agree |

## Tool to Answer Question 16

| First Name | Relationship | Hrs. Personal Contact/week | Hrs. Phone Contact/week | Things you do with | Things you do with | How Close (1-5) | | | | |
|---|---|---|---|---|---|---|---|---|---|---|
| | | | | | | 1 | 2 | 3 | 4 | 5 |
| | | | | | | | | | | |

# Bibliography

Adams, J.P. (1980). Service arrangements preferred by minority elderly: A cross-cultural survey. *Journal of Gerontological Social Work, 3* (2), 39-57.

Allen, K.R. & Chin-Sang, V. (1990). A lifetime of work: The context and meanings of leisure for aging black women. *The Gerontologist, 30* (6), 734-740.

Ball, R.E. & Robbins, L. (1986). Marital status and life satisfaction among black Americans. *Journal of Marriage and the Family, 48*, 389-394.

Billingsley, A. (1992). *Climbing Jacob's Ladder: The Enduring Legacy of African-American Families.* New York: Simon and Schuster.

Billingsley, A., & Caldwell, C.H. (1991). The church, the family, and the school in the African-American community. *Journal of Negro Education, 60*, 427-440.

Blazer, D. & Palmore, E. (1976). Religion and aging in a longitudinal panel. *The Gerontologist, 16*, 82-84.

Broman, C.L. (1988). Satisfaction among blacks: The significance of marriage and parenthood. *Journal of Marriage and the Family, 50*, 45-51.

Brook, R.H., Ware, J.E., Davies-Avery, A., Stewart, A.L., Donald, C.A., Rogers, W.H., & Johnston, S.A. (1979). Overview of adult health status measures fielded in Rand's Health Insurance Study. *Medical Care, 17*, 1-54.

Butler, R.H. & Lewis, M.I. (1982). *Aging and Mental Health: Positive Psychological and Biological Approaches.* St. Louis: Mosby.

Campbell, A., Converse, P. & Rodgers, W. (1976). *The Quality of American Life.* New York: Russell-Sage.

Cantor, M.C. (1974). Health and the inner city elderly. Paper presented at the 27th Annual Meeting of the Gerontological Society. Portland, OR.

Carter, A. (1982). Religion and the black elderly: The historical basis of social and psychological concerns. In R. Manuel (Ed.), *Minority Aging: Sociological and Social Psychological Issues.* (pp. 191-226). Westport, CT: Greenwood Press.

Chatters, L.M. & Taylor, R.J. (1989). Life problems and coping strategies of older black adults. *Social Work* (July), 313-319.

Chatters, L.M., Taylor, R.J., & Neighbors, H.W. (1989). Size of informal helper network mobilized during a serious personal problem among black Americans. *Journal of Marriage and the Family, 51,* 667-676.

Cherlin, A.J. & Furstenberg, F.F. (1986). *The New American Grandparent.* New York: Basic.

*Christianity Today* (1988). Black and white gap grows. *32* (15), p. 38.

Clavon, A. (1986). The black elderly. *Journal of Gerontological Nursing, 12* (5), 6-12.

Clavon, A. & Smith, V.P. (1986). One black couple's means of coping: Preserving integrity. *Journal of Gerontological Nursing, 12* (1), 6-12.

Coke, M.M. (1991). *Correlates of Life Satisfaction among the African-American Elderly.* New York: Garland.

Cowgill, D.O. & Holmes, L.D. (1972). *Aging and Modernization.* New York: Appleton-Century-Crofts.

Davidson, W.B. & Cotter, P.R. (1984). Sense of community identity, social networks, and psychological well-being among black and white elderly: A first look. *Journal of Minority Aging, 9* (2), 85-90.

Diener, E. (1984). Subjective well-being. *Psychological Bulletin, 95,* 977-978.

Diener, E., Emmons, R.A., Larsen, R.J. & Griffin, S. (1985). The satisfaction with life scale: A measure of global life satisfaction. *Journal of Personality Assessment, 40*, 71-75.

Dillard, J.M., Campbell, N.J., & Chisolm, G.B. (1984). Correlates of life satisfaction of aged persons. *Psychological Reports, 54,* 443-451.

Dowd, J.J. & Bengtson, V.L. (1978). Aging in minority populations: An examination of the double jeopardy hypotheses. *Journal of Gerontology, 33* (3), 427-436.

Downing, R.A. & Copeland, E.J. (1980). Services for the black elderly: National or local problems? *Journal of Gerontological Social Work, 5* (2), 127-145.

Edwards, J.N. & Klemmack, D.L. (1973). Correlates of life satisfaction: A re-examination. *Journal of Gerontology, 28,* 497-502.

Farakhan, A., Lubin, B., & O'Connor, W. (1984). Life satisfaction and depression among retired black persons. *Psychological Reports, 55,* 452-454.

Ferraro, K.F. (1980). Self-Ratings of health among the old and the old-old. *Journal of Health and Social Behavior, 20,* 45-51.

Fortes, M. (1950). *African Systems of Kinship and Marriage.* New York: Oxford University Press.

Frazier, E. F. (1966). *The Negro Family in the United States.* Chicago: University of Chicago Press.

Fullerton, J.T. & Hunsberger, B.E. (1982). A unidimensional measure of Christian Orthodoxy. *Journal for the Scientific Study of Religion, 21*, 317-326.

Gibson, R.C. (1982). Blacks at middle and late life: Resources and coping. *Annals of the American Academy of Political and Social Science, 464,* 79-90.

Gibson, R.C. (1987). Reconceptualizing retirement for black Americans. *The Gerontologist, 27* (6) 691-698.

Glazer, N. & Moynihan, D.P. (1963). *Beyond the Melting Pot.* Cambridge: MIT Press.

Gray, R.M. & Mosberg, D.O. (1977). *The church and the older person.* Grand Rapids, MI: Erdmans.

Gunter, L.M. & Kolanowski, A.M. (1986). Promoting healthy lifestyles in mature women. *Journal of Gerontological Nursing, 12,* 6-13.

Hadaway, C.K. (1978). Life satisfaction and religion: A reanalysis. *Social Forces, 57,*636-643.

Hatch, L.R. (1991). Informal support patterns of older African-American and white women: Examining effects of family, paid work, and religious participation. *Research on Aging, 13,* (2), 144-170.

Hentig, H.V. (1946). The sociological function of the grandmother. *Social Forces, 24,* 389-392.

Herskovitz, M.J. (1958). *The Myth of the Negro Past.* Boston: Beacon.

Hill, R. (1977). *Informal Adoption Among Black Families.* Washington, DC: National Urban League.

Hill, R. (1978). A demographic profile of the black elderly. *Aging,* 287-288, 297-303.

Hines, P.M. & Boyd-Franklin, N. (1982). Black families. In M. McGoldrick, J.K. Rearce, & J. Giordano (Eds.), *Ethnicity and Family Therapy.* (pp. 84-107). New York: Guilford.

Holzberg, C.S. (1982). Ethnicity and aging: Anthropological perspectives on more than just the minority elderly. *The Gerontologist, 22,* (3), 249-257.

Huling, W. E. (1978). Evolving family roles for the black elderly. *Aging, 27,* 287-288.

Hunsberger, B.E. (1985). Religion, age, life satisfaction, and perceived sources of religiousness: A study of older persons. *Journal of Gerontology, 40,* (5), 615-620.

Husaini, B.A., Moore, S.T., Castor, R.S., Neser, W., Whitten-Stovall, R., Linn, J.G., & Grifen, D. (1991). *Journal of Gerontology: Psychological Sciences, 46* (5), 236-242.

Jackson, J.J. (1970). Aged negroes: Their cultural departures from statistical stereotypes and rural-urban differences. *The Gerontologist, 10,* 140-145.

Jackson, J.J. (1971). Negro aged: Toward needed research in social gerontology. *The Gerontologist, 11,* 52-57.

Jackson, J.J. (1985). Race, national origin, ethnicity, and aging. In R.H. Binstock & E. Shanas (Eds.), *Handbook of Aging and the Social Sciences* (2nd Ed.) New York: Van Nostrand.

Kasarda, J.D. (1983). Caught in the web of change. *Society, 21,* 41-47.

Krause, N. & Tran, T.V. (1989). Stress and religious involvement among older blacks. *Journal of Gerontology: Social Sciences, 44,* 504-513.

Krishef, C.H. & Yoeling, M.L. (1981). Differential use of informal and formal helping networks among rural elderly black and white Floridians. *Journal of Gerontological Social Work, 3* (3), 45-59.

LaRue, A., Bank, B., Jarvik, L., & Hetland, M. (1987). Health in old age: How do physicians' ratings and self-ratings compare? *Journal of Gerontology, 34,* 687-691.

Lawton, M. P. (1975). The Philadelphia Geriatric Center Morale Scale: A Revision, *Journal of Gerontology,* 35, 746-757.

Liang, J. (1986). Self-reported physical health among aged adults. *Journal of Gerontology, 41* (2), 248-260.

Lincoln, C.E. & Mamiya, L.H. (1990). *The Black Church in the African-American Experience.* Durham, NC: Duke University Press.

Lindsay, I.B. & Hawkins, B.D. (1974). Research issues relating to the black aged. In L.E. Gary (Ed.), *Social Research and the Black Community: Selected Issues and Priorities.* Washington, D.C.: Institute for Urban Affairs and Research, Howard University.

Linn, M. W. & Hunter, K. I. (1979). Differences by Sex and Ethnicity in the Psychosocial adjustment of the elderly. *Journal of Health and Social Behavior,* 20, 273-281.

Linn, B.S. & Linn, M.W. (1980). Objective and self-assessed health in the old and very old. *Social Science and Medicine, 14A,* 311-315.

Lubin, B. (1981). *Depression Adjective Check Lists: Manual.* (2nd Ed.). San Diego: Educational and Industrial Testing Service.

Lund, D.A., Feinhauer, L.L., & Miller, J.R. (1985). *Journal of Gerontological Nursing, 11* (11), 29-32.

Mancini, J.A. (1981). Effects of health and income on control orientation and life satisfaction among aged public housing residents.

Manuel, R.C. (1986). A socio-demographic profile of the black aged. House Select Committee on Aging.

Markides, K.S. & Levin, J.S. (1987). The changing economy and the future of the minority aged. *The Gerontologist, 27* (3) 273-274.

McGhee, J.L. (1985). The effects of siblings on the life satisfaction of the rural elderly. *Journal of Marriage and the Family, 47,* 85-91.

Mead, M. (1970). Cultural contexts of aging. In *Twentieth-Century Faith: Hope and Survival.* New York: Harper and Row.

Mitchell, J. & Register, J.C. (1984). An exploration of family interaction with the elderly by race, socioeconomic status, and residence. *The Gerontologist, 24,* (1), 48-54.

Moore, S.T. (1991). Social density, stressors, and depression: Gender differences among the black elderly. *Journal of Gerontology, 46* (5), 236-242.

Morrisson, B.J. (1982). Sociocultural dimensions: Nursing homes and the minority aged. *Journal of Gerontological Social Work, 5* (2), 127-145.

Mossey, J.M. & Shapiro, E. (1982). Self-rated health: A predictor of mortality among the elderly. *American Journal of Public Health, 72,* 800-808.

Mutran, E. (1985). Intergenerational family support among

blacks and whites: Response of culture to socioeconomic differences. *Journal of Gerontology, 40,* 383-389.

National Urban League (1964). *Double Jeopardy: The Older Negro in America Today.* New York: National Urban League.

Neugarten, B.L., Havighurst, R.J., & Tobin, S.S. (1961). The measurement of life satisfaction. *Journal of Gerontology, 16,* 134-143.

New York City Department for the Aging (1985). *Abstract of New York City Department for the Aging's Year III of a Proposed Four-year Plan of the Older Americans Act.* New York: NYC Department for the Aging.

O'Connor, W.A., Klassen, D., & O'Connor, K.S. (1979). Evaluating human services programs: Psychological methods. In P. Ahmed & G. Coelho (Eds.), *Toward a New Definition of Health* (pp. 361-382). New York: Plenum.

Ortega, S., Crutchfield, R.D., & Rushing, W.A. (1983). Race differences in elderly personal well-being: Friendship, family, and church. *Research on Aging, 5,* 101-117.

Pearson, J.L., Hunter, A., Ensminger, M.E., & Kellam, S.G. (1990). Black grandmothers in multigenerational households: Diversity in family structure and parenting involvement in the Woodlawn community. *Child Development, 61,* 434-442.

Pfeiffer, E. (1976). *Multidimensional Functional Assessment: The OARS Methodology–A Manual.* Durham, NC: Duke University, Center for the Study of Aging and Human Development.

Quarles, B. (1987). *The Negro in the Making of America.* New York: Collier.

Radloff, L.S. (1977). The CES-D scale: A self-report depression scale for research in the general population. *Applied Psychological Measurement, 1,* 385-401.

Riley, F. (1971). Attitudes toward aging and the aged among black Americans: Some historical perspectives. *Aging and Human Development.* Vol. 3, pp. 66-70.

Rosow, I. (1967). *The Social Integration of the Aged.* New York: Free Press.

Rosow, I. (1973). The social context of the aging self. *The Gerontologist, 3,* 82-87.

Rubenstein, D.I. (1971). An examination of social participation found among a national sample of black and white elderly. *Aging and Human Development, 2,* 172-188.

Rubenstein, D.I. (1972). Social participation of aged blacks: A national sample. In J.J. Jackson (Ed.), *Proceedings of Research Conference on Minority Group Aged in the South,* October, 1971. Durham, NC: Center for the Study of Human Development and Aging, Duke University Medical Center.

Smith, J.M. (1986). Church participation and morals of the rural, southern, black aged: The effects of socioeconomic status, gender, and the organizational properties of churches. *Social Work Research and Abstracts, 22,* p. 48.

Spreitzer, E. & Snyder, E.E. (1974). Correlates of life satisfaction among the aged. *Journal of Gerontology, 29* (4), 454-458.

Steinitz, L. (1980). Religiosity, well-being, and weltanshung among the elderly. *Journal for the Scientific Study of Religion,* 19, 60-67.

Tate, L.A. (1982). Life satisfaction and death anxiety in aged women. *International Journal of Aging and Human Development, 15* (4), 299-305.

Taylor, R.J. (1985). The extended family as a source of support to elderly blacks. *The Gerontologist, 25,* 488-495.

Taylor, R.J. & Chatters, L.M. (1986). Church-based informal support among aged blacks. *The Gerontologist, 26,* 637-642.

Taylor, R.J. & Chatters, L.M. (1988). Correlates of education, income, and poverty among aged blacks. *The Gerontologist, 28* (4), 1988.

Taylor, R.J. & Chatters, L.M. (1991). Nonorganizational religious participation among elderly black adults. *Journal of Gerontology: Social Sciences, 46*(2), 5103-5111.

Taylor, R.J. & Taylor, W.H. (1982). The social and economic status of the black elderly. *Phylon, 43,* 295-306.

Taylor, R.J., Thornton, M.C., & Chatters, L.M. (1987). Black Americans' perceptions of the sociohistorical role of the church. *Journal of Black Studies, 18* (2), 123-138.

Tessler, R. & Mechanic, D. (1978). Psychological distress and perceived health status. *Journal of Health and Social Behavior, 19,* 254-262.

Tissue, T. (1974). Another look at self-rated health among the elderly. *Journal of Gerontology, 27,* 91-94.

U.S. Bureau of the Census (1983). America in transition: An aging society. *Current Population Reports,* Series P-23, No. 128. Washington, DC: U.S. Government Printing Office.

Usui, W.M. (1984). Homogeneity of friendship networks of elderly blacks and whites. *Journal of Gerontology, 39* (3), 350-356.

Usui, W.M., Keil, T.J., & Durig, K.R. (1985). Socioeconomic comparisons and life satisfaction of elderly adults. *Journal of Gerontology, 40* (1), 110-114.

Vaux, A. & Harrison, D. (1985). Support network characteristics associated with support satisfaction and perceived support. *American Journal of Community Psychology, 13,* 245-268.

Wallace, S.P. (1990a). The political economy of health for older blacks. *International Journal of Health Services, 20,* 665-680.

Wallace, S.P. (1990b). Race versus class in the health care of African-American elderly. *Social Problems, 37(4),* 517-534.

Walls, C.T. & Zarit, S.H. (1991). Informal support from black churches and the well-being of elderly blacks. *The Gerontologist, 31* (4), 490-495.

Weinberger, M., Darnell, J.C., Martz, B.L., Hiner, S.L., Neill, P., & Tierney, W.M. (1986). The effects of positive and negative life changes on the self-reported health status of elderly adults. *Journal of Gerontology, 41*(1), 114-119.

Weinberger, M., Darnell, J.C., Tierney, W.M., Martz, B.L.,

Hiner, S.L., Barker, J., & Neill, P.J. (1986). Self-rated health as a predictor of hospital admission and nursing home placement in elderly public housing tenants. *American Journal of Public Health, 76* (4), 457-459.

Wheeler, D.L. (1986). Neglected issue of aging among blacks needs more study, researchers warn. *Chronicle of Higher Education, 33*(9), 5-7.

White, D.G. (1985). *Ain't I a Woman? Female Slaves in the Plantation South.* New York: Norton.

Wright, R.W., Creecy, R.F., & Berg, W.E. (1979). The black elderly and their use of health care services: A causal analysis. *Journal of Gerontological Social Work, 2* (1), 11-29.

Wylie, F. (1971) Attitudes toward aging and the aged among black Americans. *Aging and Human Development, 3*, 66-70.

# Index

Page numbers in italics indicate figures; page numbers followed by t indicate tables.